50 Holiday Dessert Recipes

Delectable Dessert Ideas For The Christmas Holidays And Other Special Occasions

By Brianne Heaton

© Revelry Publishing 2014

Copyright 2014 by Revelry Publishing

All Rights reserved under International and Pan-American Copyright Conventions. By payment of required fees, you have been granted the non-exclusive, non-transferable right to access and read the text of this book. No part of this text may be reproduced, transmitted, downloaded, decompiled, reverse-engineered or stored in or introduced into any information storage and retrieval system, in any form or by any means, whether electronic or mechanical, now known, hereinafter invented, without express written permission of the publisher.

DISCLAIMER

All information in this book has been carefully researched and checked for factual accuracy. However, the authors and publishers make no warranty, express or implied, that the information contained herein is appropriate for every individual, situation or purpose, and assume no responsibility for errors or omissions. The reader assumes the risk and full responsibility for all actions, and the authors will not be held responsible for any loss or damage, whether consequential, incidental, special or otherwise that may result from the information presented in this publication.

We have relied on our own experience as well as many different sources for this book, and we have done our best to check facts and to give credit where it is due. In the event that any material is incorrect or has been used without proper permission, please contact us so that the oversight can be corrected.

ISBN-13: 978-0993941535
ISBN-10: 0993941532

Other books by Brianne Heaton:

51 Dump Cake Recipes: Scrumptious Dump Cake Desserts To Satisfy Your Sweet Tooth

Baking does not have to be difficult or intimidating. You can make a delicious cake in just a few steps, with just a few ingredients by using a "dump" cake recipe. Dump cakes make less mess than traditional cakes and offer unusual and decadent choices that will wow those fortunate enough to have a bite.

56 Breakfast Sandwich Recipes: Irresistible Sandwich Ideas to Kickstart Your Morning

Breakfast is the most important meal of the day so it makes sense to treat it so. Are you finding it difficult to get the right balance and variety of taste experiences every day? With breakfast sandwich mania in full swing, there is no shortage of breakfast ideas here.

51 Easter Dessert Ideas: Scrumptious Easter Recipes For Any Occasion

This holiday cookbook collection of 51 Easter dessert recipes has something tasty and enticing for everyone, and you don't have to be Julia Child in order to pull them off. The recipes can also be used for other special occasions.

46 Sriracha Flavored Recipes: Delicious Sriracha Hot Sauce Cookbook For A Spicy Palate

Check out these delectable dessert, appetizer, entree, and drink recipes and see how Sriracha can enrich even the dullest of meals. Follow our meal plan for a whole week full of delicious Sriracha meals. Your taste buds will thank you for it.

Get the latest update on new releases from the author at:

https://www.brianneheaton.com/newsletter

Table of Contents

Introduction 1
Cookies 3
    1 - Linzer Cookies 5
    2 - Coconut Orange Shortbread Cookies 7
    3 - Gingersnaps 9
    4 - M&M Cookies 11
    5 - Peppermint Thumbprints 13
    6 - Checkerboard Cookies 15
    7 - Vanillekipferl - Walnut and Vanilla Crescents 18
    8 - Snowball Cookies 20
    9 - Chocolate Crinkles 22
    10 - Royal Icing Gingerbread 24
Cakes 26
    11 - Chocolate Amaretto Cake 27
    12 - Classic Fruit Cake 29
    13 - Gingerbread Loaf 31
    14 - Sacher Torte 33
    15 - Orange Cardamom Cake 36
    16 - Mocha Yule Log 38
    17 - Marbled Loaf Cake 40
    18 - Spiced Carrot Cake 42
    19 - Cinnamon Coffee Bundt Cake 44
    20 - Lemon Poppy Seed Bundt Cake 46
Cheesecakes 48
    21 - Hot Chocolate Cheesecake 49
    22 - No Bake Orange Cheesecake 51
    23 - Chocolate Peppermint Cheesecake 53
    24 - Pumpkin Caramel Cheesecake 55
    25 - Oreo Cheesecake 58
    26 - Tiramisu Cheesecake 60
    27 - Raspberry Swirl Cheesecake 62
    28 - Cappuccino Cheesecake 64
    29 - Chocolate Peanut Butter Cheesecake 66
    30 - Cranberry Cheesecake 68
Tarts and Pies 70
    31 - Puff Pastry Apple Tart 71
    32 - Ginger Pear Galette 73

33 - Triple Chocolate Tart.. 75
34 - Linzer Tart 77
35 - Classic Apple Pie.. 79
36 - Dark Chocolate and Caramel Mini Tarts........................ 81
37 - Peanut Butter Tart.. 84
38 - Lemon Tart 86
39 - Spiced Pear and Cranberry Individual Pies 88
40 - Classic Pecan Pie 90
International Desserts.. 92
41 - Braided Sweet Bread 93
42 - Festive Tapioca Pudding 96
43 - Greek Honey Cookies... 97
44 - Mexican Bread Pudding 99
45 - Lebkuchen – German Cookies 101
46 - Viennese Whirl Cookies... 103
47 - Hamantaschen – Jewish Cookies................................. 105
48 - Apple Strudel 107
49 - Beigli – Poppy Seed Roll... 109
50 - Semolina and Almond Halva.. 111
Conclusion 113
Thank You 114
Other Books by Brianne Heaton 115
About the Author – Brianne Heaton 116
Connect with Brianne Heaton 117

Introduction

Holidays are that time of the year we spend with our family, reconnect with each other, look back on the year that went by and make wish lists for the year to come. But apart from that, holidays are the best opportunity to try new recipes, use spices and experiment with various baking ingredients. After all, what would Christmas be without your favorite cookies or that rich, luscious cheesecake you love so much? It would be incredibly boring, I tell you!

A rich chocolate cake, crumbly Linzer cookies, a dense fruit cake, a creamy pumpkin caramel cheesecake or a tangy lemon tart are all a good fit for your holiday meal table. They will elevate the meal to a whole new level of deliciousness, as well as impress your guests. After all, a meal is not complete without dessert. And that dessert has to be amazing and stand out if you want to make it a meal to remember!

This book includes 50 of the best dessert recipes fitted for your holiday meals. From cookies to cakes, cheesecake and international desserts, this book has it all. Even the pickiest eaters will find something to fit their taste. Spiced desserts or mild ones, the recipes found between these pages are well balanced and incredibly delicious while being easy enough to make without the need of any special skills. If you know how to turn on an oven then you can make these desserts, believe me!

So put your baker's apron on, line your pans with baking paper and get mixing and rolling and baking! There's no better dessert like homemade and there's no better memory like homemade desserts, especially during the emotional time that holidays are!

Delectable Dessert Ideas For The Christmas Holidays And Special Occasions

Cookies

Delectable Dessert Ideas For The Christmas Holidays And Special Occasions

1 - Linzer Cookies

Linzer cookies are a classic. They originate from the well-known Linzer tart and employ the same ingredients as the tart, but the dough is cut into cookie shapes which are then filled with jam two by two. The top cookie has a cutout shape which is also known as a Linzer eye. What you get in the end is these beautiful, gorgeous cookies filled with your favorite jam and dusted with powdered sugar to make them look festive. They are delicate and fragrant and work well with both tea and coffee, although one doesn't need an excuse to snack on a Linzer cookie.

Prep time: 2 hours
Cook time: 25 minutes
Yield: 2 dozen

Ingredients:

- 1 cup butter, softened
- $^2/_3$ cup white sugar
- 2 egg yolks
- Zest from 1 lemon
- 1 teaspoon vanilla extract

- 2½ cups all-purpose flour
- ¼ teaspoon cinnamon powder
- 1 pinch salt
- 1 teaspoon baking powder
- 1 cup almond meal (or hazelnut if you prefer)
- Raspberry jam as needed
- Powdered sugar to dust the cookies

Directions:

1. Preheat your oven to 350°F (180°C).
2. Line two baking sheets with baking paper.
3. In a bowl, mix the flour, cinnamon, salt, baking powder and almond meal.
4. In a different bowl, mix the butter and sugar until creamy and fluffy then stir in the egg yolks, one by one.
5. Add the lemon zest and vanilla then fold in the flour mixture.
6. Transfer the dough on a floured working surface and knead it a few times. Cut the dough in half and shape each piece of dough into a ball. Wrap the dough in cling film.
7. Refrigerate the dough 1 hour.
8. Unwrap the dough and place it on a floured working surface. Roll the dough into a thin sheet ($1/8$-inch or 0.3-cm thickness).
9. Cut out 2-inch (5-cm) diameter rounds with a cookie cutter. With a smaller cutter in the shape you desire, cut out the centers of half the cookies. These will be the tops.
10. Place the cookies on your prepared baking sheets and bake for 15-20 minutes until the edges begin to turn golden brown.
11. When done, remove from the oven and let them cool down in the pan.
12. Fill the cookies two by two with jam, making sure to sandwich one full cookie and one cut out cookie.
13. Dust the cookies with powdered sugar and arrange them on a platter.
14. They store well for up to 1 week in an airtight container.

Tip:

Traditionally, they are filled with raspberry jam, but there are versions of Linzer cookies filled with chocolate or even lemon curd.

2 - Coconut Orange Shortbread Cookies

Crumbly and fragrant, these cookies are tiny sweet gems, perfect for the holiday season. Not only do they look pretty, but they also taste great, combining the delicate coconut with the tangy orange and the bold chocolate. Somehow, these cookies manage to balance all these flavors into a delicious cookie!

Prep time: 35 minutes
Cook time: 35 minutes
Yield: 3 dozen

Ingredients:

- 1¼ cups all-purpose flour
- 1 pinch salt
- ¼ teaspoon baking powder
- 1 cup unsweetened shredded coconut
- ½ cup butter, softened
- ¼ cup white sugar
- 2 tablespoons orange zest
- ¼ cup fresh orange juice
- ½ teaspoon vanilla extract
- 3 oz. (85g) dark chocolate, chopped

Directions:

1. Preheat your oven to 330°F (170°C).
2. Line 2-3 baking sheets with baking paper.
3. In a food processor, combine the flour, salt, baking powder and shredded coconut.
4. Add the butter, sugar and orange zest and pulse until sandy.
5. Stir in the orange juice and vanilla and mix until a dough forms.
6. Transfer the dough on a floured working surface and roll it into a thin sheet (3-4mm thickness).
7. Cut small round cookies using a cookie cutter and place all the cookies on baking sheets.
8. Bake the cookies in the preheated oven for 15-20 minutes or until the edges begin to turn golden brown.

9. When done, remove from the oven and let them cool in the pan.
10. To coat the cookies, melt the chocolate on a double boiler or in the microwave for a few seconds.
11. Dip each cookie half way into the chocolate then place them back on the baking sheet.
12. Refrigerate until the chocolate is set then serve or store in an airtight container in a cold place. They can be stored for up to 1 week.

Tip:

Feel free to replace the orange zest with lemon or lime zest or skip it altogether and make some simple coconut cookies.

3 - Gingersnaps

Gingersnaps are a classic for the holiday season! The intense, spiced taste is what draws people to them Christmas after Christmas, but they deserve this spot due to their amazing flavor and fragrance. The outside of this cookie is sweet and crisp while the inside is moist and fragrant. Now that is what I call a perfect cookie, don't you agree?

Prep time: 30 minutes
Cook time: 25 minutes
Yield: 3 dozen

Ingredients:

- 2 cups all-purpose flour
- 2 teaspoons baking soda
- 1 teaspoon cinnamon powder
- 1 teaspoon ground ginger
- 1 pinch salt
- ¾ cup butter, softened
- 1 cup white sugar
- 1 egg
- ¼ cup molasses
- ½ teaspoon vanilla extract
- ½ cup white sugar for coating

Directions:

1. Preheat your oven at 350°F (180°C).
2. Line 2 to 3 baking sheets with baking paper and place aside.
3. Sift the flour, baking soda, salt, cinnamon and ginger in a bowl.
4. Combine the butter and sugar in a different bowl and mix until creamy.
5. Stir in the eggs, molasses and vanilla then add the flour mixture.
6. Mix well then form small dough balls.
7. Roll each dough ball through the white sugar and place them all on a baking sheet.
8. Bake for 15-20 minutes until the cookies look slightly cracked and turn slightly golden brown.

9. Let them cool in the pan then transfer in an airtight container and store for up to 4 days.

Tip:

The recipe focuses on the use of only two spices, but feel free to add more. Cardamom, nutmeg and star anise are just a few of them.

4 - M&M Cookies

M&M's are fun to eat, but what would you think about using these candies to create a colorful, delicious, crumbly cookie? It doesn't get any better, does it? The cookies are tender and the candies melt partially into the dough, infusing the cookies with its flavor.

Prep time: 20 minutes
Cook time: 25 minutes
Yield: 3 dozen

Ingredients:

- ¾ cup butter, softened
- ⅔ cup light brown sugar
- 1 egg
- ½ teaspoon vanilla extract
- 2 cups all-purpose flour
- ¼ cup cornstarch
- 1 pinch salt
- 1 teaspoon baking soda
- 4 oz. (110g) M&M candies

Directions:

1. Preheat your oven to 350°F (180°C).
2. Line two or three baking sheets with baking paper and place them aside.
3. In a bowl, sift the flour with the cornstarch, salt and baking soda.
4. In a different bowl, mix the butter and sugar until creamy and light.
5. Stir in the egg and vanilla and mix until well incorporated.
6. Add the flour and mix just until mixed well then, using a spatula, fold in the M&M candies.
7. Drop spoonsful of batter on the baking sheets making sure they are spaced out as they tend to spread.
8. Bake for 20-25 minutes or until fragrant and slightly golden brown.

9. When done, remove from the oven and let them cool down in the pan then transfer in an airtight container and store for up to 4 days.

Tip:

The M&M candies can be replaced with chocolate chips or even dried fruits, although the final cookies won't look as colorful and fun.

5 - Peppermint Thumbprints

Thumbprints are so versatile! This recipe uses peppermint candies to coat the thumbprints and the result is a crunchy, fragrant cookie with an intense chocolate taste that is well balanced by the peppermint. The cookies are filled with a rich, buttery chocolate ganache for an extra kick of flavor. But the filling does more than that – it also adds a creaminess that contrasts with the crunchy outer layer of the cookie, enhancing the taste experience.

Prep time: 1 hour
Cook time: 25 minutes
Yield: 2 dozen

Ingredients:

Cookies
- 2½ cups all-purpose flour
- ⅓ cup unsweetened cocoa powder
- 1 teaspoon baking powder
- 1 pinch salt
- 1 cup butter, softened
- 1 cup white sugar
- 1 egg
- 1 teaspoon vanilla extract
- 3 oz. (85g) Peppermint candies

Ganache filling
- 3 oz. (85g) dark chocolate, chopped
- 3 oz. (85ml) heavy cream
- 2 tablespoons butter

Directions:
1. Preheat your oven to 350°F (180°C).
2. Line two baking sheets with baking paper and place them aside.
3. Place the candies in a zip lock bag and crush them using a rolling pin into fine pieces.
4. In a bowl, sift the flour, cocoa powder, baking powder and salt.

5. In a different bowl, mix the butter and sugar until creamy and light.
6. Stir in the egg and vanilla then incorporate the flour mixture.
7. Transfer the dough on a floured working surface and knead it a few times then shape it into a ball and refrigerate 30 minutes.
8. Remove the dough from the fridge and take spoonsful of dough and shape them into small balls.
9. Roll each ball through crushed peppermint candies and place them all on baking sheets.
10. Press the center of each ball with your fingertip to make a small indentation and bake the cookies for 20-25 minutes.
11. When the cookies are done, remove the baking sheets from the oven and let them cool down in the pan.
12. For the filling, heat the cream in a saucepan then remove from heat and stir in the chocolate.
13. Mix until melted then add the butter and mix well. Let the filling cool down then fill each cookie.
14. Refrigerate the cookies to allow the filling to set then serve them or store them in an airtight container for up to 4 days.

Tip:

Replace the dark chocolate with white chocolate to create a contrast in both colors and taste.

6 - Checkerboard Cookies

The signature of these cookies is, obviously, the checkerboard pattern. They are quite impressive with their black and white pattern, but the technique to make them is quite easy. Once you get the hang of it, you can play with adding more layers. In terms of flavors, this recipe uses the two major classics: vanilla and chocolate. But lemon, orange or lavender can be added into the dough.

Prep time: 3 hours
Cook time: 25 minutes
Yield: 2 dozen

Ingredients:

Vanilla dough
- ¼ cup butter, room temperature
- ¼ cup white sugar
- 1 egg
- 1 teaspoon vanilla extract
- 1 cup all-purpose flour
- 1 pinch salt

Chocolate dough
- ¼ cup butter, softened
- ¼ cup white sugar
- 1 egg
- ½ teaspoon vanilla extract
- ¾ cup all-purpose flour
- ¼ cup cocoa powder
- 1 pinch salt
- 1 egg white, beaten

Directions:
1. To make the vanilla dough, combine all the ingredients in a food processor and pulse until a smooth dough forms.
2. Transfer the dough on a floured working surface and shape it into a ball. Wrap the dough in cling film and refrigerate at least 1 hour.
3. Repeat the same process for the chocolate dough.
4. Preheat your oven at 350°F (180°C).
5. Line two baking sheets with baking paper and place aside.
6. Unwrap the vanilla dough and place it on your floured working surface. Roll it into a thin sheet ($^1/_6$-inch or 0.4-cm thickness) then cut ½-inch (1.3-cm) strips. Place them aside.
7. Unwrap the chocolate dough as well and roll it into a thin sheet. Cut strips that have the same size as the vanilla ones.
8. Layer the strips of dough on your working surface, sealing them together with egg white. Make sure you alternate the colors to create the checkerboard pattern
9. Carefully wrap the checkerboard logs you just made in plastic wrap and freeze 15 minutes.
10. Cut the dough into ¼-inch (0.6-cm) thick slices and place them on your prepared baking sheets.
11. Bake for 15-20 minutes until the edges turn golden brown.
12. When done, remove from the oven and let them cool down in the pan before storing into an airtight container for up to 1 week.
13. A glass of milk makes a nice match for these cookies.

Tip:

Be bold and flavor the cookie dough differently. You can also play with colors by replacing the cocoa powder with flour and using a food coloring instead.

7 - Vanillekipferl - Walnut and Vanilla Crescents

Vanillekipferl originated from Vienna, Austria and are a Christmas specialty known all over Europe. However, they can be enjoyed the whole year round with a cup of tea or coffee. Their signature is the half-moon shape which is said to be celebrating the win of the Hungarian army over the Turkish army in one of the many wars between the two nations. The first thing to notice when making them is the tender, fragile dough, but it is well worth the effort of handling as the cookies are just as tender, fragrant and delicious.

Prep time: 1½ hours
Cook time: 20 minutes
Yield: 4 dozen

Ingredients:

- 1 cup butter, softened
- ½ cup powdered sugar
- 2 cups all-purpose flour
- 1 pinch salt
- 1 cup ground walnuts
- ½ cup milk
- 1 teaspoon vanilla extract
- 2 cups powdered sugar for dusting

Directions:

1. Preheat your oven at 350°F (180°C).
2. Line 4 baking sheets with baking paper and place aside.
3. Place 2 cups of powdered sugar in a bowl and place aside as well.
4. In a bowl, mix the butter and sugar until creamy and fluffy.
5. Stir in the flour, salt, walnuts, milk and vanilla and mix until well incorporated.
6. Transfer the dough on your floured working surface and shape it into a log.
7. Wrap the dough into plastic wrap and refrigerate 1 hour.
8. Unwrap the dough and place it on your working surface.

9. Take small pieces of dough (take ½ tablespoon as measurement) and shape them into thin logs or cylinders. Bend them to form a half-moon and place them on baking sheets, making sure they have enough space in between to rise.
10. Bake for 15-20 minutes until well risen and golden brown on the edges.
11. When done, remove the baking sheets from the oven and while still hot, carefully transfer the cookies into the powdered sugar.
12. Gently toss around to evenly coat the crescents then remove them from the sugar and place in an airtight container to store up to 2 weeks.

Tip:

For a different flavored cookie, replace the walnuts with hazelnuts or even almonds and use vanilla powdered sugar instead of regular.

8 - Snowball Cookies

The name of these cookies speaks for itself! They truly look like tiny snowballs made of delicious, vanilla flavored dough and plenty of powdered sugar. These cookies have Russian origins and they preserve some of the Russian spirit in the pastry world – simple, light and delicious.

Prep time: 30 minutes
Cook time: 25 minutes
Yield: 2 dozen

Ingredients:

- 1 cup butter, softened
- ¼ cup powdered sugar
- 1 teaspoon vanilla extract
- 1½ cups all-purpose flour
- ½ cup cornstarch
- 1 pinch salt
- ½ teaspoon baking powder
- 2 cups powdered sugar for dusting

Directions:

1. Preheat your oven at 350°F (180°C).
2. Line two baking trays with baking paper and place aside.
3. Place the powdered sugar in a bowl and place aside.
4. In a bowl, combine the butter and ¼ cup powdered sugar and mix until creamy and light.
5. Stir in the vanilla extract then add the flour, cornstarch, salt and baking powder.
6. Mix until the mixture comes together into a dough then transfer on your floured working surface and form small balls of dough (use 1 tablespoon as measurement).
7. Place the dough balls on baking trays and bake for 15-20 minutes just until the edges begin to turn golden brown.
8. Remove the trays from the oven and while still hot, transfer the cookies into the bowl with powdered sugar.
9. Gently toss around until the cookies are well coated with sugar.

10. Arrange the cookies on a platter or store them in an airtight container for up to 1 week.

Tip:

A variation of this recipe includes adding ground nuts into the cookie dough, but I can also picture a recipe that uses tiny bits of dried fruits as an addition into the dough.

9 - Chocolate Crinkles

What would a Christmas dessert buffet be without chocolate crinkles? These beautiful cookies are a delicacy for any chocolate lover out there! Their signature is the cracked surface covered with plenty of powdered sugar, but don't neglect the moist, rich inside either.

Prep time: 2½ hours
Cook time: 25 minutes
Yield: 2 dozen

Ingredients:

- ¼ cup butter
- 8 oz. (225g) dark chocolate (72% cocoa)
- ½ cup sugar
- 2 large eggs
- 1 teaspoon vanilla extract
- 1¾ cups all-purpose flour
- 1 pinch salt
- 1 teaspoon baking powder
- ½ cup white sugar for coating
- 1 cup powdered sugar for coating

Directions:

1. Preheat your oven to 350°F (180°C).
2. Line two baking trays with baking paper and place aside.
3. In a heatproof bowl, combine the butter and dark chocolate and place the bowl over a hot water bath. Keep the bowl over steams until the chocolate and butter are melted together.
4. Remove from heat and stir in the sugar, eggs and vanilla.
5. Add the flour, salt and baking powder and mix well then cover the batter with plastic wrap and refrigerate at least 2 hours until the dough is set.
6. Remove the bowl from the fridge and take spoonsful of dough and shape them into even balls between the palms of your hands.

7. Roll each ball of dough into granulated sugar first them into powdered sugar.
8. Place all the cookies on baking trays and bake for 15-20 minutes until cracked and slightly risen.
9. When done, remove the trays from the oven and let them cool down before serving or storing in an airtight container. They store up to 1 week.

Tip:

If you only have one baking tray available, place the dough back into the fridge between batches. Warm dough gets sticky and doesn't bake into beautiful crinkles.

10 - Royal Icing Gingerbread

Gingerbread is a Christmas staple, that's for sure! The entire world recognizes the flavors of gingerbread and loves having a bite of it on Christmas day. And truth to be told, why wouldn't they? These cookies are so pretty and fragrant that you just have to bite into them! Get your family involved into making and decorating them for a nice family moment.

Prep time: 2¼ hours
Cook time: 25 minutes
Yield: 4 dozen

Ingredients:

Gingerbread cookies
- ½ cup butter
- ½ cup white sugar
- ½ cup dark molasses
- 1 teaspoon baking powder
- 1 teaspoon baking soda
- 1 teaspoon ground ginger
- ½ teaspoon cinnamon powder
- ½ teaspoon ground cloves
- 2 cups all-purpose flour

Royal Icing
- 1 egg white
- 1½ cups powdered sugar

Directions:
1. Preheat your oven at 350°F (180°C).
2. Line your baking trays with baking paper.
3. In a bowl, mix the butter with the sugar until creamy and light. Stir in the molasses and mix well then add the remaining ingredients.
4. Transfer the dough on a floured working surface and knead a few times until the dough feels easy to work with.
5. Cut the dough in half and shape each piece into a ball.

6. Wrap the dough in cling film and place in the fridge for 1 hour.
7. After 1 hour, place the dough on your working surface and roll it into a thin sheet ($^1/_6$ inch thickness).
8. Using a cookie cutter in the desired shape, cut the dough.
9. Place the cookies on your baking trays and bake for 15-20 minutes until risen and fragrant. To check for doneness, press one cookie on the surface. It if leaves an indentation, the cookies are not done yet. If the dough doesn't sink when pressed, the cookies are done.
10. Remove the tray from the oven and allow the cookies to cool down in the pan.
11. For the royal icing, beat the egg white with the lemon juice until frothy. Add the powdered sugar and mix until the icing is thick and creamy. If needed, add more powdered sugar.
12. Spoon the royal icing into a small piping bag and decorate the cookies as you wish.

Tip:

Feel free to use sprinkles to make the cookies more colorful. To apply sprinkles, spread the royal icing over each cookie and immediately top with sprinkles. Otherwise they won't stick to the cookies.

Delectable Dessert Ideas For The Christmas Holidays And Special Occasions

Cakes

11 - Chocolate Amaretto Cake

Chocolate cake is a classic that everyone loves! But this particular recipe adds a twist to this classic – Amaretto. The intense almond taste of Amaretto gives the cake an interesting flavor that everyone will notice, but few will actually pinpoint. It's a moist, rich cake, but airy and it actually doesn't have any flour.

Prep time: 30 minutes
Cook time: 46 minutes
Servings: 8

Ingredients:

- 8 oz. (225g) dark chocolate, chopped
- ½ cup butter, cubed
- ⅔ cup white sugar
- 4 eggs, separated
- ¼ cup Amaretto
- 1 pinch salt
- 2 tablespoons cornstarch
- 1 tablespoon cocoa powder for decorating

Directions:

1. Preheat your oven at 350°F (180°C).
2. Grease a round cake pan (8-inch or 20-cm diameter) with butter and dust it with cocoa powder.
3. In a heatproof bowl, combine the butter and chocolate. Place the bowl over a hot water bath and melt them together, mixing well.
4. Remove the bowl from heat and stir in the sugar and egg yolks.
5. Add the Amaretto and cornstarch and mix well.
6. Whip the egg whites with a pinch of salt until fluffy and stiff then fold them into the chocolate mixture.
7. Pour the batter in your prepared pan and bake for 40-45 minutes. To check for doneness, insert a toothpick in the center of the cake. If it comes out clean, the cake is done, but if it still has traces of batter, keep baking a few more minutes.
8. Allow the cake to cool down in the pan before serving.
9. To serve, cover the cake with cocoa powder.

Tip:

For a nice texture contrast, top the cake before baking with sliced almonds. Once baked, they turn crisp and flavorful and pair perfectly with the Amaretto aroma of the cake.

12 - Classic Fruit Cake

Fruit cake is a Christmas treat that can be stored for quite some time. That is great because during the Christmas rush, there is so much to do, it would be nice to get some things done ahead of the holidays. This cake can be made one week ahead and stored in the fridge. Then you can either slice it and serve it or frost it with buttercream for a more festive look. It's moist and rich, loaded with flavors that are specific for Christmas – orange, dried fruits, a touch of cinnamon and dark rum.

Prep time: 1½ hours
Cook time: 1 hour
Servings: 10

Ingredients:

- ½ cup dried cranberries
- ¼ cup candied pineapple, diced
- ¼ cup candied papaya, diced
- ¼ cup candied orange peel, diced
- 1 cup golden raisins
- 1 cup dried apricots, diced
- ½ cup dark rum
- 1 cup butter, softened
- 1¼ cups sugar
- 4 eggs
- 1 teaspoon vanilla extract
- 1¼ cups all-purpose flour
- 2 teaspoons baking powder
- ½ teaspoon cinnamon powder
- 1 pinch salt

Directions:

1. Combine the cranberries, pineapple, papaya, orange peel, raisins, apricots and rum in a bowl and let them soak for 1 hour.
2. Preheat your oven to 330°F (170°C).

3. Line the bottom of a round cake pan (9.5-inch or 24-cm diameter) with baking paper and grease the sides. Set aside until needed.
4. In the bowl of your mixer, combine the butter and sugar and mix until creamy and light.
5. Add the eggs, one by one, mixing well after each addition then stir in the vanilla extract.
6. Mix in the flour, baking powder, cinnamon and salt then fold in the dried fruits, including the remaining juices.
7. Mix gently until the fruits are evenly distributed then spoon the batter into your prepared cake pan and bake for 1 hour.
8. To check if the cake is done, insert a toothpick in the center. If it comes out clean, the cake is done, but if the toothpick still has some traces of batter, the cake needs to be baked a few more minutes. Repeat the check-up a few minutes later.
9. When the cake is done, remove the pan from the oven and let it cool down in the pan.
10. Remove the cake from the pan and either serve the cake immediately or store it in the fridge, well wrapped in cling film. It stores well for up to 1 week, but if you freeze it, it can be stored for up to 3 months.

Tip:

Feel free to use your favorite dried fruits, although I recommend buying a mix of dried fruits to get as much flavor as possible.

13 - Gingerbread Loaf

This loaf is perfect for those of you who love gingerbread, but don't have the time to make tiny cookies and decorate them. The recipe takes all the flavors of gingerbread and packs them into an easy-to-make, fluffy and fragrant loaf that is easy to store and easy to serve as well. It's an amazing recipe for a quick Christmas dessert and if you serve it with a dollop of ice cream or whipped cream, you've got a stunning, exquisite treat.

Prep time: 25 minutes
Cook time: 45 minutes
Servings: 8

Ingredients:

- 1½ cups all-purpose flour
- ½ teaspoon ground ginger
- 1 teaspoon cinnamon powder
- ¼ teaspoon ground cardamom
- ¼ teaspoon ground cloves
- ¼ teaspoon all-spice
- 1 teaspoon baking soda
- 1 pinch salt
- ½ cup butter, softened
- 1 cup dark brown sugar
- ¼ cup dark molasses
- 3 eggs
- ½ cup buttermilk
- 1 teaspoon vanilla extract
- Powdered sugar to decorate

Directions:

1. Preheat your oven at 350°F (180°C).
2. Line a loaf pan with baking paper on the bottom and grease the sides with butter. Place the pan aside until needed.
3. In a bowl, sift the flour, spices, baking soda and salt.

4. In a different bowl, combine the butter and sugar and mix until creamy and light.
5. Stir in the molasses then add the eggs, one by one, mixing well after adding each of them.
6. Stir in the buttermilk and vanilla then, using a spatula, fold in the flour.
7. Spoon the batter into your prepared loaf pan and bake for 40-45 minutes until the gingerbread is well risen and fragrant.
8. When done, remove the pan from the oven and let the cake cool in the pan for 10 minutes.
9. Transfer the cake on a wire rack and let it cool down.
10. Dust with powdered sugar and serve.

Tip:

If you find the spices to be too strong, you can reduce their amount slightly or only use the ones you like the most.

14 - Sacher Torte

Sacher torte is the ultimate chocolate cake! It is a cake that not only tastes great and looks amazing in its simplicity, but it also has deep roots. There is an amazing history behind the cake which originated from Vienna. The pastry chef who invented it, Franz Sacher, also gave it its easy-to-recognize name. The cake consists of a chocolate cake filled with apricot jam and topped with a deep, rich ganache. The cake is then decorated by simply writing its name with chocolate. It is simple, but it shines with an intense chocolate taste. Once you taste it, you will surely ask for a second helping.

Prep time: 45 minutes
Cook time: 45 minutes
Servings: 8

Ingredients:

Cake
- ½ cup butter, softened
- ½ cup white sugar
- 4 egg yolks

- 6 oz. (170g) dark chocolate, melted
- ¾ cup all-purpose flour
- ½ teaspoon baking powder
- 5 egg whites
- 1 pinch salt

Chocolate glaze
- 6 oz. (170g) dark chocolate, chopped
- 1 cup heavy cream
- 1 tablespoon honey
- ½ cup apricot jam for filling
- 1 oz. (28g) white chocolate to decorate

Directions:
1. Preheat your oven to 350°F (180°C).
2. Grease a round cake pan (9-inch or 22-cm diameter) with butter and place it aside until needed.
3. To make the cake, mix the butter and sugar until creamy.
4. Stir in the egg yolks, one by one, then add the melted chocolate and mix well.
5. Stir in the flour and baking powder.
6. Whip the egg whites with a pinch of salt until stiff then using a spatula, fold the whipped egg whites into the batter.
7. Pour the batter into your prepared cake pan and bake for 40-45 minutes or until a toothpick inserted in the center of the cake comes out clean.
8. When done, remove the cake from the oven and let it cool down in the pan then transfer it on a platter and cut it in half lengthwise.
9. Spread the apricot jam between the two layers of chocolate cake.
10. To make the glaze, bring the heavy cream to the boiling point in a saucepan.
11. Remove from heat and stir in the honey then add the chocolate and mix until melted.
12. Allow the glaze to come to room temperature then pour the glaze over the cake.
13. Allow the glaze to set then melt the white chocolate and decorate the cake. Traditionally, Sacher is written on the cake.

14. Serve the cake chilled.

Tip:

Using a good quality chocolate influences the taste of the cake for the better. By good quality chocolate I mean a chocolate that has at least 70% cocoa content.

15 - Orange Cardamom Cake

Nothing says Christmas more than the aroma of fresh oranges! It's lovely how the flavor of a freshly peeled orange floods the room and your senses. And that's the same with this delicious, fragrant cake. It's moist, rich and fragrant, but also stunning in its simplicity as it is proudly displayed on your Christmas table. The twist on this recipe is the cardamom which I find to be the perfect match for orange, balancing it well.

Prep time: 25 minutes
Cook time: 45 minutes
Servings: 8

Ingredients:

Cake
- ½ cup butter, softened
- 1½ cups white sugar
- 4 eggs
- ½ cup sour cream
- 1 teaspoon vanilla extract
- 1 tablespoon orange zest
- 3 tablespoons orange marmalade
- 1½ cups all-purpose flour
- 1 teaspoon cardamom
- 1 teaspoon baking powder
- ½ teaspoon baking soda
- 1 pinch salt

Orange glaze
- 2 tablespoons fresh orange juice
- 1 cup powdered sugar
- Orange peel to decorate

Directions:
1. Preheat your oven to 350°F (180°C).
2. Line a round cake pan (9-inch or 22-cm diameter) with baking paper and place it aside until needed.

3. In the bowl of your mixer, combine the butter and sugar and mix until creamy and light.
4. Stir in the eggs, one by one, then add the sour cream, vanilla extract, orange zest and marmalade and mix well.
5. Fold in the flour, cardamom, baking powder, baking soda and salt then spoon the batter into your prepared cake pan.
6. Bake for 40-45 minutes until the cake is well risen and slightly golden brown. To check for doneness, insert a toothpick in the center of the cake. If it comes out clean, the cake is done, but if it still has traces of batter, the cake needs to be baked a few more minutes.
7. When the cake is done, remove the pan from the oven and carefully transfer the cake on a wire rack. Allow it to cool down completely before glazing it.
8. For the glaze, mix the orange juice with the powdered sugar. If the glaze is too thick, add more orange juice. If it is too thin, add more sugar until it has a consistency similar to heavy cream.
9. Drizzle the glaze over the cake and allow it to set.
10. Decorate the cake with orange peel and serve.

Tip:

If you're not a fan of orange, you can replace it with lemon, mandarin or lime.

16 - Mocha Yule Log

Yule Log is a French cake traditionally served for Christmas. The French call it *buche de Noel* because it actually looks like a wood log, although it is in fact a type of roulade filled with chocolate cream. This particular recipe takes the basic Yule Log – the shape and main ingredients - but adds a nice kick – coffee. The coffee makes the buttercream richer and gives it more aroma.

Prep time: 40 minutes
Cook time: 30 minutes
Servings: 8

Ingredients:

Sponge
- 5 eggs
- ½ cup white sugar
- ½ cup all-purpose flour
- ¼ teaspoon baking powder
- ¼ cup cocoa powder
- 1 pinch salt

Mocha buttercream
- ⅔ cup butter, softened
- 3 cups powdered sugar
- 3 oz. (85g) dark chocolate, melted and chilled
- 2 teaspoons instant coffee
- 1 teaspoon vanilla extract

Directions:

1. Preheat your oven to 350°F (180°C).
2. Line a rectangular pan (40x30cm) with baking paper and place aside until needed.
3. Sift the flour with the baking powder and cocoa.
4. To make the sponge, separate the eggs. Place the egg yolks in a bowl and the egg whites in a different bowl.

5. Whip the egg whites with a pinch of salt until stiff then gradually stir in the sugar and keep mixing until stiff and glossy.
6. Using a spatula, stir in egg yolks then fold in the flour.
7. Spoon the batter into your prepared pan and level it well.
8. Bake for 15-20 minutes until the cake springs back if pushed slightly on the surface. Do not over bake it or it will become dry and impossible to roll!
9. Remove the cake from the oven and let it cool down in the pan.
10. In the meantime, prepare the buttercream. Mix the butter with an electric mixer until creamy.
11. Gradually stir in the powdered sugar then turn the speed on high and mix until light and fluffy.
12. Stir in the melted chocolate, coffee and vanilla and mix well.
13. Split the buttercream in half.
14. Remove the sponge from the cake on your working surface. Spread one half of the buttercream over the sponge then roll it tightly into a roulade.
15. Place the rolled sponge on a platter, making sure that the edge of the sponge is underneath.
16. Cover the cake with the remaining buttercream and refrigerate 10 minutes.
17. Using a fork, trace a pattern over the roll and place back in the fridge to allow it to completely set.
18. Slice and serve the cake chilled, dusted with powdered sugar to resemble snow.

Tip:

The coffee is not compulsory and you can replace it with vanilla, orange, rum or just leave it simple to taste the chocolate better.

17 - Marbled Loaf Cake

This marbled cake is absolutely beautiful with the contrasting black and white patter! The recipe itself is pretty simple and basic, but the pattern makes it shine. It is like a surprise cake – you don't expect much looking at it from the outside, but when you slice through it, you discover amazing colors and a rich taste of vanilla and chocolate.

Prep time: 30 minutes
Cook time: 45 minutes
Servings: 8

Ingredients:

- 5 eggs
- 1 pinch salt
- 1 cup white sugar
- 1½ cups all-purpose flour
- 1 teaspoon baking powder
- ¼ cup vegetable oil
- 1 teaspoon vanilla extract
- 2 tablespoons cocoa powder
- 3 tablespoons water

- Powdered sugar to decorate

Directions:
1. Preheat your oven to 350°F (180°C).
2. Line a loaf pan with baking paper or grease it with butter and place it aside until needed.
3. Sift the flour with baking powder in a bowl.
4. Separate the egg yolks.
5. Mix the egg whites with a pinch of salt until stiff, then gradually stir in the sugar and mix until the whites are stiff and glossy.
6. In a small bowl, combine the egg yolks, oil and vanilla and mix well.
7. Combine the egg yolks with the whipped whites and mix gently until completely incorporated.
8. Gradually fold in the sifted flour then split the batter in half.
9. Mix the cocoa powder with the water until smooth then combine this mixture with one half of batter and mix gently.
10. To form the batter, take your loaf pan and spoon the batter into the pan, layering two tablespoons of vanilla batter with two tablespoons of chocolate batter.
11. Continue layering them until you run out of batter.
12. Bake the cake for 40-45 minutes. To check for doneness, press the cake with your fingertip. If it springs back, the cake is done. If it sinks, bake the cake a few more minutes and check again.
13. When done, remove from the oven and allow the cake to cool in the pan.
14. Serve the loaf dusted with powdered sugar if you prefer.

Tip:

If you prefer, you can replace the cocoa powder with a pinch of food coloring, thus creating a colored marble cake. In fact, you can be adventurous and split the batter into more portions and color each portion in a different color.

18 - Spiced Carrot Cake

Carrot cake is well known all around the world and people have a different approach to it – some love it, some hate it. But in the end, it is a rich, moist, spiced cake that's worth trying at least once in your lifetime. This particular recipe yields a fragrant cake, topped with the most delicious and airy cream cheese frosting, flavored with plenty of vanilla and a touch of lemon zest to make it more vibrant and lighter.

Prep time: 45 minutes
Cook time: 45 minutes
Servings: 8

Ingredients:

Cake
- 4 eggs
- 1½ cups white sugar
- 1 cup vegetable oil
- 2 cups all-purpose flour
- 2 teaspoons baking soda
- 1 pinch salt
- 1 teaspoon cinnamon powder
- ½ teaspoon ground cardamom
- 1 pinch nutmeg
- 1 tablespoon orange zest
- 3 cups grated carrots
- ½ cup walnuts, chopped
- ½ cup golden raisins
- 1 cup crushed pineapple, drained

Cream cheese frosting
- ¼ cup butter, softened
- 1½ cups cream cheese, room temperature
- 4 cups powdered sugar
- 2 teaspoons vanilla extract
- Orange peel and walnut halves to decorate

Directions:
1. Preheat your oven to 350°F (180°C).
2. Line two identical round cake pans (9.5-inch or 24-cm diameter) with baking paper and place them aside until needed.
3. In a large bowl, mix the eggs and sugar until creamy and triple in volume.
4. Stir in the vegetable oil then fold in the flour, baking soda, salt, cinnamon, cardamom and nutmeg.
5. Using a spatula, fold in the grated carrots, walnuts, raisins and pineapple then split the batter in half and pour it into the prepared pans.
6. Bake for 30-40 minutes or until the cake springs back when pressed slightly. When done, the cake will also be golden brown and fragrant.
7. Remove the pans from the oven and let the cakes cool down in the pan.
8. For the frosting, mix the butter until creamy and light then stir in the cream cheese and mix well.
9. Add the sugar, ½ cup at a time, and mix well after each addition.
10. Turn your mixer on high and mix it 5 additional minutes until fluffy and light.
11. Add the vanilla and mix well.
12. To finish the cake, place one carrot sponge on a platter. Top with a good dollop of cream cheese frosting and cover with the remaining frosting.
13. Decorate the cake simple, with walnut halves and orange peel.

Tip:

The batter is quite versatile and can be customized to your taste. The pineapple can be skipped and replaced with more carrots. Coconut flakes can be added as well and the spices can be replaced or skipped. It's all about experimenting and finding your favorite combination.

19 - Cinnamon Coffee Bundt Cake

Despite its name, this cake contains no coffee. Instead, the coffee refers to a technique of combining the batter with layers of cinnamon streusel in this cake. It is a moist, fragrant cake, quite impressive in terms of flavor profile which makes it perfect for the holiday season. What makes this cake moist and delicious is the addition of sour cream in the batter. The cream keeps the moisture in the cake and makes it rich and flavorful.

Prep time: 30 minutes
Cook time: 45 minutes
Servings: 10

Ingredients:

Streusel
- ¼ cup all-purpose flour
- ½ cup sugar
- 2 teaspoons cinnamon powder
- 2 tablespoons chilled butter
- 1 cup walnuts, chopped

Cake
- 4 large eggs
- 1½ cups sour cream
- 1 teaspoon vanilla extract
- 3 cups all-purpose flour
- 1 pinch salt
- 1 teaspoon baking powder
- 1 teaspoon baking soda
- 1 cup white sugar
- 1 cup butter, softened

Directions:
1. Preheat your oven to 350°F (180°C).
2. Grease a large Bundt cake pan with butter and place it aside until needed.

3. Make the streusel by combining all the ingredients together in a bowl. Rub them well with your fingertips until sandy and place aside.
4. For the cake, in a bowl, mix the eggs with half of the sour cream and vanilla.
5. In a different bowl, combine the flour, salt, baking powder, baking soda and sugar then stir in the butter and remaining sour cream.
6. Add the egg and cream mixture and mix well with an electric mixer.
7. Spoon ¼ of the batter into your Bundt cake pan and top with a few spoonsful of streusel. Add a new layer of batter and top with streusel again. Continue to do so until you run out of batter and streusel.
8. Bake the cake for 45 minutes or until well risen and golden brown.
9. When done, remove from the oven and let the cake cool down in the pan.
10. Transfer the cake on a platter and slice it chilled.

Tip:

Walnuts have an intense, rich nut taste, but you can also use pecans or cashews and even the slightly more delicate almonds.

20- Lemon Poppy Seed Bundt Cake

Lemon and poppy seeds are a match made in heaven! The tangy and fragrant lemon balances the slightly bitter, crunchy poppy seed perfectly, creating a cake that not only tastes great, but also looks amazing. It's a refreshing cake, but rich at the same time and I find it to be one of the best desserts after a rich Christmas meal.

Prep time: 20 minutes
Cook time: 45 minutes
Servings: 10

Ingredients:

- 2½ cups all-purpose flour
- 2 teaspoons baking powder
- ½ teaspoon baking soda
- 1 pinch salt
- 1 cup butter, softened
- 1¼ cups white sugar
- 4 eggs
- 1 teaspoon vanilla extract
- Juice and zest from 1 lemon
- 1 cup buttermilk
- 2 tablespoons poppy seeds
- Powdered sugar to decorate

Directions:

1. Preheat your oven to 350°F (180°C).
2. Grease a large Bundt pan with butter and place aside until needed.
3. Sift the flour, baking powder, baking soda and salt in a bowl and place aside.
4. In a different bowl, mix the butter and sugar until creamy and light.
5. Stir in the eggs, one by one, then add the vanilla extract, lemon juice and lemon zest.
6. Begin adding the flour, alternating it with buttermilk. Always begin with flower and end with flour.

7. Mix the batter just until well incorporated then fold in the poppy seeds.
8. Spoon the batter into your Bundt pan and bake for 45 minutes.
9. To check if the cake is done, insert a toothpick in the center. If the toothpick comes out clean, the cake is done, but if the toothpick still has traces of batter, bake the cake a few more minutes.
10. When the cake is done, remove the pan from the oven and allow it to cool for 10 minutes.
11. Turn the cake upside down on a wire rack and let it cool completely.
12. Dust with powdered sugar and serve.

Tip:

The lemon flavor is not compulsory. Lime, mandarin, orange or bergamot can be used instead.

Delectable Dessert Ideas For The Christmas Holidays And Special Occasions

Cheesecakes

21 - Hot Chocolate Cheesecake

Nothing compares to a rich, creamy hot chocolate cheesecake! What makes this cake special is the use of hot cocoa mix which gives it a lot of flavor and makes it creamier and richer. It is a cheesecake designed for the chocoholics with its chocolate crust and filling. The chocolate glaze is the cherry on top, turning the cheesecake into one of the most delicious desserts you will ever taste.

Prep time: 30 minutes
Cook time: 1 hour
Servings: 10

Ingredients:

Crust
- 1½ cups crushed chocolate biscuits
- ¼ cup butter, melted

Filling
- 32 oz. (900g) cream cheese, softened
- ½ cup heavy cream
- 1 cup white sugar

- ½ cup hot cocoa mix
- 4 eggs
- 1 teaspoon vanilla extract
- 1 pinch salt

Topping
- 4 oz. (115g) milk chocolate, chopped
- 3 oz. (85ml) heavy cream
- 1 tablespoon butter

Directions:
1. Preheat your oven to 330°F (170°C).
2. Line a round cake pan (10.5-inch or 26-cm diameter) with baking paper and place aside until needed.
3. To make the crust, mix the ingredients in a food processor and pulse until well combined.
4. Transfer the biscuits into your prepared cake pan and press them well on the bottom of the pan.
5. For the filling, mix the cream cheese, heavy cream, sugar, hot cocoa mix, eggs, vanilla and salt in a bowl and mix well.
6. Pour the filling over the crust and bake for 1 hour.
7. When the cheesecake is done, remove from the oven and let it cool down in the pan.
8. Carefully transfer the cheesecake on a platter.
9. For the topping, pour the cream in a saucepan and bring it to the boiling point.
10. Remove from heat and stir in the chocolate. Mix until melted then incorporate the butter.
11. Allow the topping to cool slightly then pour it over the cheesecake.
12. Refrigerate the cheesecake for 1 hour before serving.

Tip:

For an extra dose of chocolate, add ½ cup chocolate chips or chocolate chunks into the filling mixture.

22 - No Bake Orange Cheesecake

This no bake cheesecake tastes more like an exquisite cake than a cheesecake. It is refreshing and creamy and has an intense citrus taste that will flood your senses with each bite. The orange jelly on top is the perfect finish for such a delicious cheesecake and you don't even have to turn your oven on for this. How great is that?

Prep time: 2 hours
Cook time: 10 minutes
Servings: 8

Ingredients:

Crust
- 1 cup graham crackers
- ½ cup cashew nuts
- 2 tablespoons butter, melted

Filling
- 2 cups cream cheese, softened
- 8 oz. (230g) mascarpone cheese, softened
- 1 cup powdered sugar
- 1 teaspoon vanilla extract
- 1 tablespoon orange zest
- 1 cup heavy cream, whipped
- 1½ teaspoons gelatin
- ¼ cup fresh orange juice

Orange topping
- 1½ cups fresh orange juice
- 1 teaspoon orange zest
- 1½ teaspoons gelatin

Directions:

1. Line a round cake pan (9.5-inch or 24-cm diameter) with parchment paper and place it aside.
2. To make the crust, combine all the ingredients in a food processor and pulse until ground and well combined.

3. Transfer the mixture into your prepared pan and press it well on the bottom of the pan. Place the pan in the fridge.
4. For the filling, first bloom the gelatin in ¼ cup fresh orange juice.
5. In a bowl, combine the cream cheese with mascarpone, sugar, vanilla and orange zest and mix well.
6. Melt the gelatin in the microwave for 10 seconds and stir it into the cheese mixture.
7. Fold in the whipped cream then pour the filling over the crust and place back in the fridge.
8. To make the orange topping, mix the gelatin with ½ cup orange juice and let it bloom for 10 minutes.
9. Bring the remaining orange juice to the boiling point then stir in the orange zest and remove from heat.
10. Strain the mixture through a fine sieve and stir in the bloomed gelatin.
11. Allow the mixture to cool to room temperature then gently pour it over the cheesecake.
12. Place the cheesecake in the fridge for at least 1 hour then unmold and transfer the cheesecake on a platter.
13. Serve the cheesecake chilled.

Tip:

The orange can easily be replaced with other fruits, such as passion fruit and lemon or peaches and lemon. It's a versatile recipe so be bold and experiment until you find the combination that you enjoy the most.

23 - Chocolate Peppermint Cheesecake

The holidays wouldn't be the same without the combination between chocolate and peppermint! It's what I call a contrasting combination, but it's precisely that contrast between the rich chocolate and refreshing peppermint that makes this cheesecake such a delicacy. The mint aroma floods your senses with every bite and the chocolate mellows it down perfectly.

Prep time: 30 minutes
Cook time: 1 hour
Servings: 8-10

Ingredients:

Crust
- 30 chocolate biscuits
- ½ cup melted butter
- 1 tablespoon milk

Filling
- 24 oz. (680g) cream cheese, softened
- 1 cup heavy cream
- 8 oz. (230g) dark chocolate chips
- 1 cup white sugar
- 4 eggs
- 1 pinch salt
- 1 teaspoon peppermint extract
- 2 tablespoons melted butter

Directions:
1. Preheat your oven to 330°F (170°C).
2. Line a round cake pan (9.5-inch or 24-cm diameter) with baking paper and place aside until needed.
3. To make the crust, place the biscuits in a food processor and pulse until ground.
4. Stir in the butter and milk and mix well then transfer the mixture into your prepared cake pan and press it well on the bottom and sides of the pan. Place aside.

5. For the filling, pour the heavy cream into a small saucepan and bring to the boiling point.
6. Remove from heat and stir in the chocolate. Mix until melted.
7. Transfer the chocolate into a bowl then stir in the cream cheese, sugar, eggs, salt, peppermint and butter. Mix until the filling is smooth.
8. Pour the filling into the crust and bake for 1 hour or until the center of the cheesecake looks set.
9. When done, remove the pan from the oven and allow the cheesecake to cool in the pan.
10. Serve the cheesecake filled.

Tip:

For an extra taste of peppermint, add ¼ cup crushed peppermint candies into the filling.

24 - Pumpkin Caramel Cheesecake

The earthy, fragrant pumpkin and the rich, buttery caramel sauce are a match made in heaven for exquisite palates. You can appreciate the intense flavor of the filling and the way it combines with the walnut crust and rich caramel sauce. The spices used are the final touch and they turn this cheesecake into a real delicacy. One serving won't be enough for you or your guests, be certain of that!

Prep time: 45 minutes
Cook time: 1 hour
Servings: 10

Ingredients:

Crust
- 15 graham crackers
- ½ cup walnuts
- 2 tablespoons pumpkin seeds
- 2 tablespoons brown sugar
- 3 tablespoons melted butter

Filling
- 28 oz. (800g) cream cheese, softened
- 1 cup pumpkin puree
- 1 cup sugar
- ½ teaspoon cinnamon powder
- ½ teaspoon ground ginger
- 1 pinch nutmeg
- 1 pinch salt
- 5 eggs
- 1 teaspoon vanilla extract

Caramel sauce
- 1 cup white sugar
- ¼ cup brown sugar
- 1 cup heavy cream
- 1 pinch salt

Directions:
1. Preheat your oven to 330°F (170°C).
2. Line a round cake pan (9.5-inch or 24-cm diameter) with baking paper and place it aside until needed.
3. To make the crust, combine the crackers, walnuts, sugar and pumpkin seeds in a food processor and pulse until ground.
4. Stir in the melted butter and mix until combined.
5. Transfer the mixture into your cake pan and press it well on the bottom of the pan. Place aside.
6. For the filling, combine the cream cheese, pumpkin puree, sugar, spices, salt, eggs and vanilla in a bowl and mix until smooth.
7. Pour the filling over the crust and bake for 50-60 minutes.
8. To check if the cheesecake is done, gently shake the pan. If the center of the cheesecake looks set, it's done. If the center looks wobbly, liquid, bake a few more minutes and check again.
9. When the cheesecake is done, remove the pan from the oven and let the cheesecake cool in the pan.
10. Transfer the cheesecake on a platter.
11. To make the caramel sauce, combine the white sugar and brown sugar in a heavy saucepan and melt over medium flame until it has an amber color.

12. Stir in the heavy cream and keep over heat until smooth and melted. Be careful as it might foam up.
13. Remove the caramel from heat and stir in the butter. Allow the caramel to cool then pour it over the cheesecake.
14. Serve the cheesecake chilled.

Tip:

Decorate the cheesecake with walnut halves.

25 - Oreo Cheesecake

Who doesn't love Oreos? We all adore them, but how about a cheesecake that uses these amazing biscuits to make the crust then adds a few crushed biscuits into the filling as well? You will love the delicious, exceptional crust and creamy, delicate filling. It's easy to make and absolutely scrumptious!

Prep time: 2 hours
Cook time: 10 minutes
Servings: 8

Ingredients:

Crust
- 15 Oreo cookies
- ¼ cup melted butter

Filling
- 24 oz. (680g) cream cheese, softened
- 1 cup sour cream
- 2 eggs
- 4 egg yolks
- ¾ cup white sugar
- 1 pinch salt
- 1 teaspoon vanilla extract
- 12 Oreo cookies, chopped into smaller pieces
- Oreo cookies to decorate

Directions:
1. Preheat your oven to 330°F (170°C).
2. Line a round cake pan (9.5-inch or 24-cm diameter) with baking paper and place aside until needed.
3. To make the crust, place the Oreos in a food processor and pulse until ground.
4. Add the melted butter and mix well then transfer the mixture into your prepared pan and press it well on the bottom and sides of the pan.

5. For the filling, combine the cream cheese, sour cream, eggs, egg yolks, sugar, salt and vanilla in a bowl and mix well.
6. Fold in the crushed Oreos and pour the filling into the crust.
7. Bake for 1 hour until the center of the cheesecake looks set.
8. When done, remove the pan from the oven and allow the cheesecake to cool in the pan before transferring it on a serving platter.
9. Decorate with Oreos and serve chilled.

Tip:

If you are not a fan of Oreos, feel free to replace them with Amaretti cookies and add a touch of Amaretto liqueur into the filling as well.

26 - Tiramisu Cheesecake

If you are a coffee fan, this recipe is for you! The creamy, delicate mascarpone filling and coffee aroma is a match made in heaven. Simply top the cheesecake with a sprinkling of cocoa powder before serving and you've got yourself a delicious, exquisite dessert that will end your Christmas meal on a high note.

Prep time: 25 minutes
Cook time: 55 minutes
Servings: 8-10

Ingredients:

Crust
- 25 Biscoff cookies
- ¼ cup melted butter
- 1 tablespoon Kahlua liqueur

Filling
- 24 oz. (680g) cream cheese, softened
- ½ cup heavy cream
- 3 eggs
- 2 egg yolks
- 1 pinch salt
- ⅔ cup white sugar
- ¼ cup Kahlua liqueur
- 2 teaspoons instant coffee
- Cocoa powder to decorate

Directions:
1. Preheat the oven to 330°F (170°C).
2. Line a round baking pan (9.5-inch or 24-cm diameter) with baking paper and place it aside.
3. To make the crust, crush the biscuits in a food processor then add the butter and liqueur and mix until well combined.
4. Transfer the mixture into your prepared pan and press it well on the bottom of the pan.

5. For the filling, combine all the ingredients into a bowl and mix well.
6. Pour the filling over the crust and bake for 55 minutes or more. To check for doneness, gently shake the pan. If the center doesn't look wobbly, the cheesecake is done.
7. Remove the pan from the oven and allow the cheesecake to cool completely in the pan.
8. Transfer the cheesecake on a platter and decorate with cocoa powder.
9. Serve the cheesecake chilled.

Tip:

This recipe is not recommended for kids due to the addition of liqueur, but feel free to skip adding it if you're looking for a lighter version.

27 - Raspberry Swirl Cheesecake

This beautiful cheesecake will put a smile on everyone's face! It looks stunning and it tastes just as good! The delicate raspberry swirl pairs perfectly with the vanilla cream cheese filling, creating a dessert that will end your holiday meal on a high note. What I love about this recipe is that it can be made into individual servings as well, it's incredibly easy to adapt and much easier to serve as a miniature cheesecake.

Prep time: 30 minutes
Cook time: 1 hour
Servings: 8-10

Ingredients:

Crust
- 1½ cups graham crackers, crushed
- ¼ cup butter, melted

Filling
- 2 pounds (900g) cream cheese, softened
- 4 eggs

- 1 pinch salt
- 1½ teaspoons vanilla extract
- 1 cup white sugar

Raspberry swirl
- 1 cup fresh or frozen raspberries
- 1 teaspoon lemon juice
- 2 tablespoons white sugar
- 1 tablespoon cornstarch

Directions:
1. Preheat your oven to 330°F (170°C).
2. Line a round cake pan (10.5-inch or 26-cm diameter) with baking paper and place it aside.
3. To make the crust, mix the crushed crackers with butter and rub the mixture well until well combined. Transfer the crackers in your prepared pan and press them well on the bottom of the pan.
4. To make the filling, combine all the ingredients in a bowl and mix well.
5. Pour the filling over the crust and place the pan aside.
6. To make the raspberry swirl, puree the raspberries, lemon juice, cornstarch and sugar in a blender.
7. Pass the mixture through a fine sieve if you don't like the seeds.
8. Drop spoonsful of raspberry mixture into the filling then using a fork, swirl the raspberry mixture until you get a mixed patter.
9. Bake for 1 hour then remove the cheesecake from the oven and let it cool in the pan.
10. Serve the cheesecake chilled, topped with a few berries as decoration.

Tip:

Replace the raspberries with strawberries or blueberries.

28 - Cappuccino Cheesecake

This cheesecake has a delicate flavor of coffee and it is rich, creamy and luscious! The chocolate crust is the perfect match for the moist cappuccino filling. A slice of this cheesecake is the perfect end to a hardy Christmas meal and it will impress even the fussiest guests with its incredible taste and delicate aroma.

Prep time: 20 minutes
Cook time: 1 hour
Servings: 8-10

Ingredients:

Crust
- 25 chocolate biscuits
- ½ cup butter, melted
- 1 tablespoon powdered sugar
- 1 tablespoon cocoa powder

Filling
- 20 oz. (560g) cream cheese, softened
- 1 cup sour cream
- 1 can (14 oz. or 354g) sweetened condensed milk
- 4 eggs
- 1 teaspoon vanilla extract
- 3 tablespoons instant espresso coffee
- 1 pinch salt

Directions:

1. Preheat your oven to 330°F (170°C).
2. Line a round cake pan (9.5-inch or 24-cm diameter) with baking paper and place it aside until needed.
3. To make the crust, crush the biscuits into a food processor. Add the sugar, cocoa and melted butter and mix until well combined.
4. Transfer the mixture into your prepared pan and press it well on the bottom of the pan.
5. For the filling, mix all the ingredients in a bowl.

6. Pour the filling over the crust and bake for 1 hour.
7. To check for doneness, shake the pan gently. If the center is wobbly, the cheesecake is not done yet. Bake a few more minutes until the center looks set.
8. When done, remove the pan from the oven and allow the cheesecake to cool before slicing and serving.

Tip:

The condensed milk is enough to sweeten the filling, but feel free to add sugar if you want the cheesecake sweeter. I would recommend brown sugar for a touch of extra flavor.

29 - Chocolate Peanut Butter Cheesecake

This cheesecake combines two of the most loved ingredients across the globe – chocolate and peanut butter. This combination needs no introduction! It's the perfect mix of sweet, salty and slightly bitter and it manages to balance these flavors so well that it can get addictive.

Prep time: 25 minutes
Cook time: 1 hour
Servings: 8-10

Ingredients:

Crust
- 30 chocolate biscuits
- ½ cup melted butter

Filling
- 24 oz. (680g) cream cheese, softened
- ½ cup sour cream
- 1 cup smooth peanut butter
- 2 tablespoons melted butter
- ½ cup brown sugar
- ¼ cup white sugar
- 3 eggs
- 1 teaspoon vanilla extract

Topping
- 3 oz. (85g) dark chocolate, chopped
- 2 oz. (60ml) heavy cream

Directions:
1. Preheat your oven to 330°F (170°C).
2. Line a round cake pan (10-inch or 25-cm diameter) with baking paper and place it aside until needed.
3. To make the crust, place the biscuits in a food processor and pulse until ground.

4. Add the butter and mix well then transfer the mixture into your prepared pan and press it well on the bottom and sides of the pan. Place aside.
5. For the filling, mix the cream cheese with the peanut butter then add the remaining ingredients and mix well.
6. Pour the filling into the crust and bake for 1 hour until the center of the cheesecake looks set.
7. When done, remove from the oven and allow the cheesecake to cool completely.
8. For the topping, bring the cream to the boiling point in a small saucepan. Remove from heat and stir in the chocolate.
9. Mix until melted and smooth then allow the mixture to come to room temperature and drizzle it over the cheesecake.
10. Chill the cheesecake until serving.

Tip:

For a milder taste, skip the chocolate topping. The cheesecake will have a less intense taste, but still preserve its creaminess and richness.

30 - Cranberry Cheesecake

Holiday meals are hardy so after such a meal, you may just want a refreshing, light dessert to awaken your senses. And this cheesecake is precisely that – a creamy, tangy, refreshing dessert, perfect to end a meal on the highest possible note. The cranberry topping is the secret to this delicious cheesecake. It's the topping that makes this dessert as outstanding as it is!

Prep time: 30 minutes
Cook time: 55 minutes
Servings: 8-10

Ingredients:

Crust
- 1 cup blanched almonds
- 1 cup graham crackers
- ¼ cup melted butter
- 2 tablespoons honey

Filling
- 24 oz. (680g) cream cheese, softened
- 1 cup sour cream
- ¼ cup honey
- ¼ cup white sugar
- 3 eggs
- 2 egg yolks
- 1 pinch salt
- 1 teaspoon vanilla extract

Topping
- 1 cup fresh cranberries
- ¼ cup fresh orange juice
- 2 tablespoons sugar
- 1 teaspoon gelatin

Directions:

1. Preheat your oven to 330°F (170°C).

2. Line a round cake pan (10.5-inch or 26-cm diameter) with parchment paper and place it aside until needed.
3. To make the crust, place the almonds and crackers in a food processor. Pulse until ground then stir in the butter and honey.
4. Pulse until well mixed then transfer the mixture into your prepared pan and press it well on the bottom and sides of the pan.
5. To make the filling, combine all the ingredients in a bowl and mix well.
6. Pour the mixture into your crust and bake for 55 minutes.
7. When done, remove the pan from the oven and allow it to cool completely before transferring it on a platter.
8. For the topping, bloom the gelatin in fresh orange juice for 10 minutes then melt it in the microwave for 10 seconds.
9. Puree the cranberries with the sugar in a blender then stir in the melted gelatin.
10. Drizzle the topping over the cheesecake and refrigerate until serving.

Tip:

The cranberries, although recommended, are not compulsory. You can replace them with strawberries, blueberries or a mix of berries for an invigorating taste.

Delectable Dessert Ideas For The Christmas Holidays And Special Occasions

Tarts and Pies

31 - Puff Pastry Apple Tart

This simple and quick apple tart is a delicacy! The ingredient list is so short that it's hard to believe you can create such a delicious dessert with just two main ingredients. But that's the beauty of this recipe – it takes two common ingredients and combines them in the easiest way to create a crisp, rich, buttery tart. This recipe is particularly good if you've got guests at the last moment and need a quick dessert fix!

Prep time: 15 minutes
Cook time: 20 minutes
Servings: 6-8

Ingredients:

- 1 sheet puff pastry, thawed
- 6 medium size apples
- ½ lemon, juiced
- 1 egg, beaten
- ½ cup brown sugar
- ½ teaspoon cinnamon powder
- Powdered sugar to serve

Directions:

1. Preheat your oven to 375°F (190°C).
2. Line two baking sheets with baking paper.
3. Peel and core the apples then cut them into thin slices. Sprinkle the apples with lemon juice to prevent them from turning brown and mix them with half of the sugar.
4. Unwrap and place the puff pastry dough on your working surface.
5. Cut the dough into two equal pieces and place each piece on a separate baking sheet.
6. Top each piece of dough with apple slices, leaving the edges clear.
7. Brush the dough on the edges with egg then sprinkle the tart with the leftover sugar and cinnamon.
8. Bake for 20-25 minutes or until puffed up and golden brown.
9. When done, remove the tart from the oven and let it cool completely before serving.
10. Dust with powdered sugar to decorate.

Tip:

To make sure the tart puffs up perfectly, bake it at high heat. The high heat will force the dough to release steam and rise.

32 - Ginger Pear Galette

Galette is an easy-to-make kind of pie that takes less time than a traditional pie, but preserves the same taste and crisp crust. It's a versatile dessert. Although this particular recipe uses pears and ginger as flavoring, you can make a galette using other combinations of fruits and spices, such as apples, cinnamon, berries, and vanilla. The sky is the limit!

Prep time: 30 minutes
Cook time: 30 minutes
Servings: 6-8

Ingredients:

- 1½ cups all-purpose flour
- 2 tablespoons white sugar
- ¼ teaspoon baking powder
- 1 pinch salt
- ½ cup chilled butter, cubed
- 2-4 tablespoons cold water
- 4 ripe pears, cored and sliced
- ¼ teaspoon cinnamon powder
- ½ teaspoon ground ginger
- 2 tablespoons brown sugar
- 1 egg yolk for egg wash
- 1 tablespoon brown sugar for sprinkling

Directions:

1. Prehcat your oven to 350°F (180°C).
2. Line a baking sheet with baking paper and place aside until needed.
3. In a food processor, combine the flour, white sugar, baking powder, salt and butter and pulse until sandy.
4. Add the chilled water, 1 tablespoon at a time, and pulse until it comes together into a dough.
5. Transfer the dough on your working surface and knead it a few times then roll it into an even round if possible, about ¼-inch (0.6-cm) thickness.

6. Transfer the dough on your baking sheet.
7. In a bowl, mix the pear slices with the cinnamon, ginger and brown sugar then place the pears over the dough, leaving the edges clear.
8. Fold the edges of the dough over the pears, leaving the center exposed.
9. Brush the dough with egg yolks and sprinkle with brown sugar
10. Bake for 25-30 minutes until the top is golden brown and the pears look tender and juicy.
11. When done, remove from the oven and allow the galette to cool before slicing and serving.

Tip:

For an exquisite dessert, slice the galette while still slightly warm and top it with a dollop of ice cream as garnish when serving.

33 - Triple Chocolate Tart

For chocolate lovers out there, this recipe is for you! The triple dose of chocolate makes this tart rich and deep, but it's so delicious that you won't be able to stop at just one slice. The crisp crust and creamy topping is a match made in heaven! I recommend using a dark chocolate that has at least 60% cocoa content to make sure your tart has an intense taste and the right consistency.

Prep time: 30 minutes
Cook time: 1 hour
Servings: 8-10

Ingredients:

Crust
- 20 chocolate graham crackers
- ½ cup butter, melted
- 2 tablespoons powdered sugar

Filling
- 1½ cups heavy cream
- ¼ cup honey
- 10 oz. (280g) dark chocolate, chopped
- 2 eggs
- 1 egg yolk
- 1 teaspoon vanilla extract
- 1 pinch salt

Glaze
- ½ cup heavy cream
- 2 oz. (55g) dark chocolate, chopped
- 1 oz. (28g) butter

Directions:
1. Preheat your oven to 350°F (180°C).
2. To make the crust, place the crackers in a food processor and pulse until ground.

3. Add the sugar and butter and mix well then transfer the mixture into a round tart pan and press it well on the bottom and sides of the pan.
4. Bake the crust 15 minutes.
5. To make the filling, pour the cream in a saucepan and bring it to the boiling point.
6. Remove from heat and stir in the honey. Mix until melted then add the chocolate and mix until smooth and completely melted.
7. Stir in the eggs, egg yolk, vanilla and salt and mix well.
8. Pour the filling into the crust and place the pan back in the oven.
9. Reduce the heat to 330°F (170°C) and bake for 35-40 minutes. Turn your oven off and let the tart in the oven for 15 additional minutes.
10. When done, remove the pan from the oven and allow it to cool completely.
11. To make the topping, bring the cream to the boiling point in a saucepan. Remove from heat and stir in the chocolate and butter and mix until melted.
12. Allow the glaze to come to room temperature then pour it over the filling.
13. Refrigerate until serving.

Tip:

Adding a pinch of salt mellows down the taste of chocolate and balances it perfectly. Salt is the key to amazing chocolate desserts!

34 - Linzer Tart

Just like Linzer cookies, this tart has Austrian roots. In fact, the tart is the original and the cookies were created later. The signature of this dish is the nutty, buttery crust filled with raspberry jam, topped with the same delicious, nutty dough. Traditionally, the tart is topped with a lattice, but it takes time to master the perfect lattice so feel free to use your own, custom design to decorate it. In the end, it will still be a delicious, rich tart.

Prep time: 1 hour
Cook time: 40 minutes
Servings: 8-10

Ingredients:

Crust
- 1 cup blanched almonds
- 1 cup peeled hazelnuts
- 1½ cups all-purpose flour
- ½ cup white sugar
- 1 teaspoon lemon zest
- 1 cup butter, softened
- 2 egg yolks
- 1 whole egg
- 1 teaspoon vanilla extract

Filling
- 2 cups raspberry preserve

Directions:

1. Preheat your oven to 350°F (180°C).
2. Place the almonds and hazelnuts in a food processor and pulse until ground.
3. Add the flour, sugar and lemon zest and mix well.
4. Stir in the butter, egg yolks, egg and vanilla and pulse until the dough comes together.

5. Transfer the dough on your floured working surface and knead it a few times then split the dough in half and shape each portion into a round.
6. Wrap the dough in plastic wrap and refrigerate 30 minutes.
7. Unwrap half of the dough and place it on a floured working surface.
8. Roll the dough into a thin sheet and place it in your tart pan. Press the dough well on the bottom and sides of the pan and trim the edges if needed.
9. Spread the raspberry preserve into the crust.
10. Unwrap the remaining dough and roll it into a thin sheet as well.
11. At this point you can either make the traditional lattice or simply cut out shapes of dough with a cookie cutter and place them over the tart. That's the simplest way and creates stunning results.
12. Bake the tart for 40 minutes until the edges and top begin to turn golden brown.
13. Serve the tart chilled.

Tip:

The raspberry preserve, although traditional, is not compulsory and it can be replaced with orange jam, cherry preserve or any other combination you prefer.

35 - Classic Apple Pie

Nothing beats a slice of this classic apple pie when it comes to comfort desserts! The crisp, flaky crust and juicy, delicious filling are out of this world. It's amazing how something as common as apples can turn into such a delicious dessert. This recipe is perfect as it is – it relies more on the tartness and freshness of apples rather than using too many spices. What you get is a dessert that will please even the pickiest eaters!

Prep time: 30 minutes
Cook time: 1 hour
Servings: 8-10

Ingredients:

Crust
- 2 cups all-purpose flour
- ½ teaspoon baking powder
- 1 pinch salt
- ⅔ cup chilled butter, cubed
- 2-4 tablespoons cold water

Filling
- 2 pounds (900g) cooking apples, peeled and sliced
- ½ cup white sugar
- 1 tablespoon cornstarch
- ½ teaspoon cinnamon powder
- ½ teaspoon ground ginger
- 1 egg yolk for egg wash
- 2 tablespoons brown sugar to sprinkle

Directions:

1. Preheat your oven to 350°F (180°C).
2. Slightly grease a pie pan with butter and place it aside until needed.
3. To make the crust, combine the flour, baking powder, salt and butter in a food processor.

4. Pulse until the mixture is sandy then add the cold water, one tablespoon at a time and pulse until it comes together into an even dough.
5. Transfer the dough on your working surface and split it in half.
6. Roll one half of dough into a thin sheet (¼-inch or 0.6-cm thickness) and place it into your pie pan, pressing the dough well on the bottom and sides of the pan.
7. Trim off the edges if needed.
8. For the filling, combine the apple slices, white sugar, cornstarch, cinnamon and ginger in a bowl and mix them well.
9. Transfer the filling into the crust.
10. Roll out the remaining dough and top the filling.
11. Seal the edges well and cut a few holes into the top layer of dough to allow the steams to come out.
12. Brush the pie with egg wash and sprinkle with brown sugar.
13. Bake for 50-60 minutes or until the pie is golden brown and fragrant.
14. When done, remove the pie from the oven and let it cool in the pan before slicing and serving.

Tip:

The twist on this recipe could be adding a scoop of ice cream when serving. I recommend vanilla or ginger ice cream because it complements the apples better.

36 - Dark Chocolate and Caramel Mini Tarts

The chocolate crust, caramel filling and chocolate glaze are a match made in heaven. It's hard to forget this sweet, rich, delicious combination! Once you bite into one of these tarts, the caramel oozes out and you will want a second bite right away.

Prep time: 1 ¼ hours
Cook time: 25 minutes
Servings: 12

Ingredients:

Crust
- ⅔ cup butter, softened
- ¼ cup powdered sugar
- 2 eggs
- 2 cups all-purpose flour
- ½ cup cocoa powder
- 1 pinch salt
- ½ teaspoon baking powder

Caramel sauce
- 1 cup sugar
- ½ cup heavy cream
- 1½ oz. (40g) butter

Glaze
- ⅔ cup heavy cream
- 6 oz. (170g) dark chocolate, chopped

Directions:
1. Preheat your oven to 350°F (180°C).
2. Prepare your mini tart pans and place them aside.
3. To make the crust, mix the butter with sugar until creamy and light then stir in the eggs, one by one.
4. Add the flour, cocoa powder, salt and baking powder and mix until the dough comes together nicely.
5. Transfer the dough on a floured working surface and knead it a few times then shape it into a round and wrap it in plastic wrap.
6. Refrigerate the dough for 30 minutes.
7. Unwrap the dough and place it on a floured working surface. Roll the dough into a thin sheet ($\frac{1}{6}$-inch or 0.4-cm thickness) then cut circles of dough and place them in your prepared tart tins.
8. Press the dough on the bottom and sides of the pans.
9. Bake the mini tart crusts for 15-20 minutes or until the edges begin to turn golden brown.
10. Remove the crusts from the oven and let them cool in the pan.
11. To make the caramel sauce, melt the sugar in a heavy saucepan until it has an amber color.
12. Stir in the heavy cream, being careful as it foams up. Keep cooking the sauce until smooth then remove from heat and stir in the butter. Mix until melted then allow the sauce to cool.
13. Pour the sauce into the tart crusts and place in the fridge until the glaze is ready.
14. To make the glaze, bring the cream to the boiling point in a small saucepan.
15. Remove from heat and stir in the chocolate. Mix until melted.
16. Pour the glaze over the caramel and refrigerate until set.
17. Serve the tarts chilled.

Tip:

For extra texture and taste, add chopped hazelnuts in the caramel sauce.

37 - Peanut Butter Tart

Who doesn't love peanut butter? This tart brings peanut butter desserts to a whole new level by combining it with a crisp, salty crust and a chocolate glaze. The final tart is exceptional and has a scrumptious taste that can easily get addictive. However, despite its richness, it's an airy dessert that melts in your mouth with each bite.

Prep time: 40 minutes
Cook time: 25 minutes
Servings: 8-10

Ingredients:

Crust
- 2 cups pretzels
- ½ cup melted butter

Peanut butter mousse
- 1 cup cream cheese, softened
- 1 cup peanut butter
- ½ cup brown sugar
- 1 teaspoon vanilla extract
- 1 cup heavy cream, whipped

Glaze
- 4 oz. (115g) milk chocolate, chopped
- 1 oz. (30g) dark chocolate, chopped
- ⅔ cup heavy cream
- 2 tablespoons butter

Directions:
1. Preheat your oven to 350°F (180°C).
2. To make the crust, place the pretzels in a food processor and pulse until ground.
3. Stir in the melted butter and mix well then transfer the mixture into a tart pan and press it well on the bottom and sides of the pan.
4. Bake the tart for 15-20 minutes until fragrant and golden brown.

5. When done, remove from the oven and let the crust cool in the pan.
6. To make the peanut butter mousse, mix the cream cheese, peanut butter and brown sugar in a bowl.
7. Stir in vanilla then fold in the whipped cream.
8. Spoon the mousse into the chilled crust and refrigerate until the glaze is ready.
9. To make the glaze, pour the cream in a saucepan and bring it to the boiling point.
10. Remove from heat and stir in the chocolate. Mix until melted then stir in the butter.
11. Allow the glaze to cool to room temperature then pour the glaze over the mousse.
12. Refrigerate until set then slice and serve.

Tip:

The salty pretzels combine perfectly with the peanut butter and chocolate, but if you're not too fond of the taste, feel free to use regular graham crackers instead.

38 - Lemon Tart

This tangy, refreshing tart is the best dessert to end a holiday meal. The fragrant, intense taste of lemon balances the richness of a holiday meal perfectly. Top the tart with whipped cream and you've got yourself an exquisite, delicious dessert.

Prep time: 1 hour
Cook time: 45 minutes
Servings: 8-10

Ingredients:

Crust
- 1¼ cups all-purpose flour
- ¼ cup powdered sugar
- 1 pinch salt
- ½ cup chilled butter, cubed
- 1 teaspoon lemon zest
- 2-4 tablespoons cold water

Filling
- 1 can (14 oz. or 354g) sweetened condensed milk
- ½ cup lemon juice (125ml)
- 2 tablespoons lemon zest
- 2 eggs
- 2 egg yolks
- ½ teaspoon vanilla extract

Topping
- 1½ cups heavy cream
- ½ cup powdered sugar
- 1 teaspoon vanilla extract

Directions:

1. Preheat your oven to 350°F (180°C).
2. To make the crust, mix the flour, sugar and salt in a food processor.
3. Add the butter and lemon zest and mix until sandy.

4. Stir in the water, one tablespoon at a time, and mix until it comes together.
5. Transfer the dough on a floured working surface and knead it a few times. Wrap the dough in plastic wrap and refrigerate 30 minutes.
6. Unwrap and place the dough on your working surface.
7. Roll the dough into a thin sheet ($^1/_6$-inch or 0.4-cm thickness) and transfer it on your tart pan. Press the dough on the bottom and sides of the pan and bake the crust for 15 minutes.
8. Remove the crust from the oven and place aside.
9. To make the filling, combine all the ingredients in a bowl and mix well.
10. Pour the filling into the crust and place the pan back into the oven.
11. Turn the heat to 330°F (170°C) and bake for 40 more minutes until set.
12. When done, remove the pan from the oven and let it cool in then pan.
13. To make the topping, whip the cream with sugar until stiff. Stir in the vanilla extract.
14. Top the tart with whipped cream and serve it chilled.

Tip:

You can replace the lemon with lime or other citrus fruit to create a whole new recipe.

39 - Spiced Pear and Cranberry Individual Pies

Individual pies are delicious, juicy and easy to make, especially this particular recipe! The pears turn tender and the cranberries burst into delicious pieces of juicy fruits. What you get is crisp, puffed up tiny individual pies, perfect for a holiday buffet. The flavors of these pies are a holiday match as well!

Prep time: 30 minutes
Cook time: 20 minutes
Servings: 10

Ingredients:

- 1 sheet puff pastry dough
- 4 pears, peeled, cored and diced
- 1 cup fresh or frozen cranberries
- ¼ teaspoon cinnamon powder
- ¼ cup brown sugar
- ¼ teaspoon ground ginger
- 1 egg, beaten

Directions:

1. Preheat your oven to 375°F (190°C).
2. In a bowl, mix the pears, cranberries, cinnamon, sugar and ginger.
3. Place the puff pastry dough on your working surface and cut into squares.
4. Place 1-2 tablespoons of filling in the center of each square. Brush the edges with egg then fold the squares in half to form a triangle.
5. Seal the edges by slightly pressing them and place the pies on a baking sheet lined with parchment paper.
6. Brush the pies with egg wash and bake for 20 minutes or until puffed up and golden brown.
7. When done, remove from the oven and let them cool down in the pan before serving.

Tip:

Replace the pears with apples, pumpkin cubes or even berries. It's a versatile recipe that can be customized in any way you like. Even savory fillings are amazing!

40 - Classic Pecan Pie

Nothing comes close to a pecan pie when it comes to flavor to fit the holidays. Pecans, maple syrup, cinnamon and ginger come together to create a rich, intense pie. The crisp crust and delicious pecans flooded by a sweet and sticky filling are the perfect Christmas dessert for anyone with a sweet tooth.

Prep time: 30 minutes
Cook time: 1 hour
Servings: 8-10

Ingredients:

Crust
- ½ cup butter, softened
- ¼ cup powdered sugar
- 1 egg yolk
- 1½ cups all-purpose flour
- 1 pinch salt
- ½ teaspoon baking powder

Filling
- ½ cup maple syrup
- 1 cup golden syrup
- 3 eggs
- ¼ cup butter, melted
- ½ teaspoon vanilla extract
- ½ teaspoon cinnamon powder
- ¼ teaspoon ground ginger
- 10 oz. (280g) pecan halves
- 1 pinch salt

Directions
1. Preheat your oven to 350°F (180°C).
2. To make the crust, mix the butter and sugar in a bowl until creamy.
3. Stir in the egg yolk then add the flour, salt and baking powder and mix well.

4. Transfer the dough on a floured working surface and knead until it comes together. Add more flour if the dough is sticky.
5. Roll the dough into a thin sheet ($1/6$-inch or 0.4-cm thickness) and place it in a tart pan. Press the dough well on the bottom and sides of the pan and trim off the edges if needed.
6. Place a baking sheet over the dough and fill the crust with dried beans. This is called blind baking and it is done to ensure an even, well baked crust.
7. Bake the crust for 20 minutes until it begins to turn golden brown then remove from the oven and place it aside until the filling is done.
8. For the filling, mix the maple syrup, golden syrup and eggs until frothy.
9. Stir in the melted butter, vanilla, cinnamon, ginger and salt then fold in the pecans.
10. Pour the filling into the crust then place the pan back in the oven. Turn the heat to 330°F (170°C) and bake the pie for 40 minutes until set.
11. Remove from the oven and let it cool completely before slicing and serving.

Tip:

A chocolate crust would bring this tart to a whole new level of deliciousness and it's incredibly easy to make as well. Replace part of the flour in the crust recipe with cocoa powder and it's done!

Delectable Dessert Ideas For The Christmas Holidays And Special Occasions

International Desserts

41 - Braided Sweet Bread

This braided sweet bread has Romanian roots, although similar versions can be found in other East European countries as well. It is a sweet bread filled with a chocolate and walnut mixture and braided usually using two strands, although three or four strands are possible too, just more difficult to handle. What you get is delicious sweet bread that can be paired with a glass of cold milk or a cup of hot tea.

Prep time: 2 hours
Cook time: 1 hour
Yield: 2 loaves

Ingredients:

Sweet bread
- 2 pounds (900g) all-purpose flour
- 1 pinch salt
- 4 eggs
- 2 egg yolks
- 1 cup warm milk
- 1 cup sugar

- 1 teaspoon vanilla extract
- 1 tablespoon lemon zest
- 3 teaspoons instant active yeast
- ½ cup butter, melted
- ½ cup vegetable oil

Filling
- 2 egg whites
- ½ cup sugar
- ½ cup cocoa powder
- 1 cup ground walnuts
- 1 egg for egg wash

Directions:
1. To make the dough, in a bowl, sift the flour and salt.
2. In a different bowl, mix the eggs, egg yolks, sugar, vanilla, lemon zest and yeast. Pour this mixture over the flour and mix well.
3. Knead the dough for a few minutes then begin adding the melted butter and oil, gradually, spoon after spoon, kneading well. The key to fluffy, delicious bread is kneading it for at least 30 minutes until the dough is elastic and easy to work with.
4. Cover the bowl with a clean kitchen towel and let the dough rise for 40 minutes.
5. Line two loaf pans with baking paper and place aside.
6. Preheat your oven to 350°F (180°C).
7. Make the filling by whipping the egg whites with sugar until stiff.
8. Stir in the cocoa powder and walnuts and mix well.
9. Transfer the dough on your floured working surface and cut it in two equal portions.
10. Take one half of dough and cut it in two once more. Roll each piece of dough into a ½-inch or 1.3-cm thick rectangle. Evenly spread half of the walnut filling on both pieces of dough, and then roll each of them tightly. The next step is to braid the two rolls then place the bread into your prepared pans.
11. Repeat with the remaining dough.
12. Place the pans aside and let them rise for 30 additional minutes.

13. Brush each sweet bread with egg wash.
14. Bake for 45 minutes or until well risen and golden brown.
15. Allow the bread to cool in the pan before slicing and serving.
16. A glass of milk makes a nice match for this braided sweet bread.

Tip:

Although traditionally this recipe is made with a walnut and chocolate filling, other versions use cream cheese or even Nutella or other types of chocolate spreads. Often, Turkish delight is added in the filling to sweeten it up and flavor it.

42 - Festive Tapioca Pudding

Tapioca is a type of starch mostly used in the Southern part of the American continent, especially Brazil. It is similar to rice in taste and the way it is cooked, but even if it's such a simple and basic ingredient, people still cook it as part of their traditional holiday meal. It is versatile enough to be cooked into exquisite desserts so expect to see it on your Christmas table.

Prep time: 10 minutes
Cook time: 30 minutes
Servings: 6

Ingredients:

- 1 cup tapioca pearls, rinsed
- 1½ cups coconut milk
- 1 cup eggnog
- 1 pinch nutmeg
- ¼ cup white sugar
- 1 cup whipped cream to serve
- 1 oz. (28g) dark chocolate, chopped to decorate

Directions:

1. In a heavy saucepan, mix the tapioca pearls, coconut milk, eggnog and nutmeg and bring to a boil over low heat.
2. Cook for 15 minutes then stir in the sugar and cook 5 additional minutes.
3. Pour the pudding into individual serving glasses and let it cool completely before serving.
4. To serve, top with whipped cream and garnish with a few chocolate bits.

Tip:

If you replace the eggnog with coconut milk, you get a pudding that can be served any time of the year for breakfast or as a treat for your kids.

43 - Greek Honey Cookies

Greek desserts are simple and most of them revolve around the amazing flavor of honey, which is healthier than sugar after all. These cookies combine honey with olive oil and almonds and are tender and absolutely delicious. The sweetness is quite intense, but that's the Greek way of making desserts – they are sweet and filling and you can't really have more than 2 or 3 cookies at a time.

Prep time: 45 minutes
Cook time: 25 minutes
Yield: 4 dozen

Ingredients:

Cookies
- 1 cup olive oil
- ¾ cup white sugar
- 1 tablespoon orange zest
- 1 cup orange juice
- 1 tablespoon orange liqueur (optional)
- ½ teaspoon baking soda
- 1 pinch nutmeg
- 1 pinch ground cloves
- 4 cups all-purpose flour
- ½ cup ground almonds
- 1 pinch salt

Honey glaze
- ½ cup honey
- ⅓ cup water
- 1 cinnamon stick
- 1 star anise
- 1 cup sliced almonds to garnish

Directions:
1. Preheat your oven to 350°F (180°C).

2. Line your baking sheets with baking paper and place aside until needed.
3. To make the cookies, in a large bowl, mix the oil with sugar, orange zest, orange juice and liqueur if using any.
4. Mix well then stir in the baking soda, nutmeg, ground cloves, flour, almonds and salt.
5. Mix well to form a dough. Transfer the dough on your floured working surface. Take spoonsful of dough and form small balls.
6. Place the cookies on your prepared baking sheets and flatten them slightly with the back of a spoon.
7. Bake for 15 minutes until the edges begin to turn golden brown.
8. When done, remove from the oven and let the cookies cool in the pan.
9. To make the glaze, combine the honey, water, cinnamon and star anise in a small saucepan and bring to a boil.
10. Remove from heat and allow the glaze to cool to a temperature that you can handle.
11. Dip each cookie into the honey glaze then quickly roll it through sliced almonds.
12. Place the cookies on a platter and serve.

Tip:

The sliced almonds may be not always stick on the cookies due to their size so prior to glazing the cookies, crush the almond slices with a rolling pin into smaller pieces.

44 - Mexican Bread Pudding

It is well known that Mexicans don't like wasting food and they've found so many creative ways of using leftovers! This includes bread which is may be the most basic food we eat, but it can easily turn into an incredibly delicious dessert. And this Mexican recipe sure knows how to accomplish that! The secret of this recipe is the cheese topping, but don't underestimate the combination. The sweet bread pudding and gooey, salty topping couldn't taste any better than that! This pudding is usually made for Christmas in most Mexican homes and it's a huge hit.

Prep time: 30 minutes
Cook time: 50 minutes
Servings: 8

Ingredients:

- 6 cups bread cubes (1 day old bread preferred)
- 1 cup dark brown sugar
- 1 cup water
- 1 cup coconut milk
- 2 eggs
- ½ teaspoon cinnamon powder
- ½ cup golden raisins
- ½ cup sliced almonds
- 2 tablespoons butter, cut into small pieces
- ½ cup grated Monterey Jack cheese

Directions:

1. Preheat your oven to 350°F (180°C).
2. Slightly grease a deep baking pan with butter.
3. Place the bread cubes into the pan.
4. In a bowl, combine the sugar, water, coconut milk, eggs, cinnamon and raisins in a bowl.
5. Pour this mixture over the bread and mix gently until the bread soaks up all the liquid.
6. Top with almonds, butter pieces and grated cheese and bake for 50 minutes until the top is golden brown and crusty.

7. Serve the bread pudding warm or chilled.

Tip:

The cheese topping is what makes this pudding special so do not skip it! Try this particular recipe at least once then decide if you like it or not.

45 - Lebkuchen – German Cookies

These German cookies are similar to gingerbread and are traditionally made in Germany, although it is a recipe that has been adapted and used in many other countries across Europe. The cookies are crumbly and fragrant and the spices used are perfect for holidays so there's no wonder people love them. In addition to this, they store well for up to 2 weeks in an airtight container.

Prep time: 30 minutes
Cook time: 25 minutes
Yield: 4 dozen

Ingredients:

Cookies
- 2½ cups all-purpose flour
- ½ cup ground almonds
- 1 teaspoon ground ginger
- ½ teaspoon cinnamon powder
- 1 teaspoon baking soda
- ½ teaspoon baking powder
- 1 pinch salt
- ½ cup honey
- 1 tablespoon lemon zest
- ½ cup butter, melted

Glaze
- 1 egg white
- 1 cup powdered sugar

Directions:

1. Preheat your oven to 350°F (180°C).
2. Line your baking sheets with baking powder and place aside until needed.
3. To make the cookies, sift the dry ingredients in a bowl.
4. Combine the honey, lemon zest and butter in a small saucepan and heat the mixture up until melted.

5. Pour the mixture over the flour and mix well. Knead the dough until it comes together and it looks elastic.
6. Using your hands, roll out the dough into 30-40 balls and place them all on your prepared baking sheets. Flatten the cookies with the palm of your hand and bake for 20-25 minutes or until the edges turn golden brown.
7. While the cookies bake, mix the egg white with the sugar to form a runny glaze.
8. Remove the cookies from the oven and while still hot, drizzle them with the sugar glaze.
9. Let them cool in the pan then store in an airtight container for up to two weeks.

Tip:

If you'd like more glaze, double the recipe and dip the cookies completely into the glaze. The heat of the cookies will set the glaze almost instantly.

46 - Viennese Whirl Cookies

The signature of these cookies is the double layer of butter cookie filled with buttercream and raspberry jam. These cookies are true gems of the Viennese pastry cuisine! They taste amazing, but what is impressive is their unique look. The golden cookies, the bright red filling and fluffy buttercream look great layered together!

Prep time: 40 minutes
Cook time: 20 minutes
Yield: 2 dozen

Ingredients:

Cookies
- 1 cup butter, softened
- ½ cup powdered sugar
- 1 teaspoon vanilla extract
- 1 cup all-purpose flour
- ½ cup corn flour (cornstarch)
- 2 tablespoons milk

Buttercream

- ¼ cup butter, room temperature
- 1½ cups powdered sugar
- 1 teaspoon vanilla extract
- ⅔ cup raspberry jam to fill the cookies

Directions:

1. Preheat your oven to 375°F (190°C).
2. Line your baking sheets with baking paper and place aside until needed.
3. To make the cookies, combine all the ingredients in a food processor and pulse until the batter is smooth and creamy without overworking it.
4. Spoon the batter into a pastry bag fitted with a large nozzle tip and pipe small rosettes on your prepared baking sheets.
5. Bake the cookies for 15-20 minutes or until the edges turn golden brown.
6. Remove the baking sheets from the oven and allow the cookies to cool completely.
7. To make the buttercream, mix the butter and sugar in a bowl until creamy. Stir in the sugar and mix at least 5 minutes until fluffy and light. Stir in the vanilla extract.
8. Spoon the buttercream into a pastry bag fitted with a small star nozzle.
9. Spread raspberry jam on each cookie then fill them two by two with piped buttercream.
10. Place them on a platter and chill them until the filling is set.
11. They store in the fridge for up to 4 days.

Tip:

This recipe is incredibly versatile. Once you have the whirls done, you can mix and match the filling from a simple vanilla buttercream to a chocolate or coffee one. Step out of tradition, experiment and find a version that suits your taste better!

47 - Hamantaschen – Jewish Cookies

These cookies are traditionally made for the Jewish holidays, but they are so good that it would be a shame not to give them a chance even if you're not Jewish. Their signature is the triangular shape and fruit filling, usually made with a delicate jam of your choice. The dough is made with cream cheese which lends it a flaky and rich texture, perfect for a holiday treat.

Prep time: 40 minutes
Cook time: 25 minutes
Yield: 2 dozen

Ingredients:

- 4 oz. (115g) cream cheese, room temperature
- ²/₃ cup butter, softened
- ¼ cup white sugar
- ½ teaspoon vanilla extract
- 1½ cups all-purpose flour
- 1 pinch salt
- ¼ teaspoon baking powder
- ½ cup apricot jam

Directions:

1. Preheat your oven to 375°F (190°C).
2. Line two baking sheets with baking paper and place aside until needed.
3. In a bowl, combine the butter and cream cheese then add the sugar and mix until creamy and light.
4. Stir in the vanilla extract then add the flour, salt and baking powder.
5. Mix well then transfer the dough on a floured working surface and knead it a few times to bring it together.
6. Roll the dough into a thin sheet (¹/₆-inch or 0.4-cm thickness) then using a round cookie cutter not larger than 3 inches, cut the dough into rounds.
7. Place the dough rounds on your baking sheets.

8. Place ½ teaspoon apricot jam in the center of each dough round then fold the edges all the way around to form a triangle.
9. Bake for 15-20 minutes or until the cookies begin to turn slightly golden brown.
10. Remove the baking sheets from the oven when done and allow the cookies to cool in the pan before serving.

Tip:

For a different taste, replace the apricot jam with raspberry jam or orange marmalade. You could get even more adventurous and use lemon jam with poppy seeds or a cream cheese mixture, although prunes are often used in the most traditional Jewish kitchens.

48 - Apple Strudel

Although strudel has Austrian roots, nowadays it has become a worldwide dessert that's gained its popularity due to its tantalizing taste and ease of making. With phyllo dough sheets available at every supermarket, it is now even easier to enjoy a slice of strudel for the holidays or whenever you feel like indulging in a juicy, fragrant dessert.

Prep time: 30 minutes
Cook time: 45 minutes
Servings: 10-12

Ingredients:

- 1 package phyllo dough sheets
- ¼ cup melted butter
- 6 apples, peeled, cored and diced
- ½ cup golden raisins
- 2 tablespoons lemon juice
- 2 tablespoons dark rum
- ¼ cup brown sugar
- 1 tablespoon cornstarch
- 1 teaspoon lemon zest
- ½ teaspoon cinnamon powder

Directions:

1. Preheat your oven to 350°F (180°C).
2. Line a baking sheet with parchment paper and place it aside until needed.
3. In a bowl, combine the apples, raisins, lemon juice, rum, sugar, cornstarch, lemon zest and cinnamon.
4. Open your phyllo dough package and unwrap it on your working surface.
5. Layer the phyllo dough sheets on your baking sheet, brushing each of them with melted butter.
6. Spread the apple filling over the phyllo sheets then carefully wrap the dough tightly.

7. Bake the strudel for 40-45 minutes or until golden brown and crisp.
8. When done, remove from the oven and allow it to cool completely before slicing and serving.

Tip:

Traditionally, the strudel is served with ample vanilla custard. The vanilla custard adds creaminess and aroma, but also makes it more festive.

49 - Beigli – Poppy Seed Roll

Beigli is a traditional Hungarian dessert usually filled with a poppy seed cream, although some recipes use a walnut filling instead. Beigli is a mix of sweet bread and a roll and it tastes delightful and looks spectacular. You won't see a Hungarian Christmas table without it as it is embedded deep in the cuisine of the nation… and why wouldn't it? It is comfort food at its best!

Prep time: 1 ½ hours
Cook time: 45 minutes
Yield: 2 loaves

Ingredients:

Dough
- 1 cup warm milk
- 2 teaspoons active dry yeast
- ¼ cup white sugar
- 2 egg yolks
- 2 eggs
- 1 cup butter, melted
- 3½ cups all-purpose flour
- 1 pinch salt

Filling
- 2 cups poppy seeds
- 2 tablespoons lemon zest
- ¼ cup honey
- 2 tablespoons melted butter
- 1 egg for egg wash

Directions:

1. To make the dough, combine the milk, yeast and sugar in a large bowl and let it bloom for 5 minutes.
2. Stir in the egg yolks, eggs and butter then add the flour and salt.

3. Mix well then knead the dough until elastic and easy to work with.
4. Cover the dough with a clean kitchen towel and let it rise for 30 minutes.
5. Preheat your oven to 350°F (180°C).
6. Transfer the dough on a floured working surface and cut it in half.
7. Roll each piece of dough into a ½-inch or 1.3-cm thick rectangular sheet.
8. Spread the poppy seed filling over each piece of rolled dough then carefully roll the dough.
9. Transfer the rolls on a baking sheet and brush them with egg wash.
10. Bake for 40-45 minutes or until golden brown and well risen.
11. When done, remove the rolls from the oven and let them cool in the pan.
12. Slice and serve.

Tip:

For an extra crunch, top the rolls with brown sugar just before baking. The sugar will melt, caramelize and create a crunchy topping that enhances the flavor and texture.

50 - Semolina and Almond Halva

The halva is a sweet mix of various ingredients, traditionally made in the Asian part of the world. There are dozens of halva recipes and versions out there, many of them using fruits or vegetables as a base. But none of them is as filling and flavorful as this semolina and almond halva. It's rich and yet delicate and can be molded into various cups to give it a more festive look. With a serving of this you will get a taste of Asian cuisine!

Prep time: 10 minutes
Cook time: 20 minutes
Servings: 4

Ingredients:

- 1 cup semolina
- ½ cup ground almonds
- 2 oz. (55g) sliced almonds
- 2 oz. (30g) ghee
- 2 ½ cups milk
- ½ cup brown sugar
- ½ cinnamon stick
- 2 cardamom pods, crushed

Directions:

1. Place the semolina and ground almonds in a skillet and roast them slightly over medium flame. Be careful not to burn them! All you want is a subtle roasted aroma.
2. Remove the skillet from heat and place aside.
3. Combine the ghee, milk, sugar, cinnamon and cardamom in a heavy saucepan and bring to a boil over medium flame.
4. Stir in the semolina and almonds and cook for 15-20 minutes, mixing all the time with a wooden spoon as it tends to stick to the bottom of the pan.
5. It is done when most of the liquid has been absorbed and it is fragrant and has a brown color.
6. Spoon the halva into small individual molds or ramekins and refrigerate until chilled.

7. To serve, turn the molds upside down on plates and top with slices almonds.

Tip:

Ghee is a type of Asian butter that has been clarified by melting and cooking it slightly. The idea is to remove any milk or cream residues and be left with only the fat found in the butter.

Conclusion

Don't let these holidays pass by without making any homemade desserts! They definitely are the ultimate desserts in terms of flavor and taste – comfort food at its highest!

Your family will surely appreciate a rich chocolate cake or a peanut butter tart or maybe their own favorite if you're feeling confident enough! That is what the holidays are all about, whether it's Christmas, Easter or Thanksgiving – loving each other and showing it even if it's through small gestures like baking something for your family or friends!

Make the time you share with your family and friends a memorable one with scrumptious desserts to top it all off.

Thank You

If you enjoyed the recipes, please consider leaving a review of the book. Good reviews encourage an author to write as well as help books to sell. Good reviews can be just a few short sentences describing what you liked about the book. If you could spend 30 seconds writing a review, I would appreciate it. You can review this title right now at your favorite retailer.

Other Books by Brianne Heaton

- 51 Dump Cake Recipes: Scrumptious Dump Cake Desserts To Satisfy Your Sweet Tooth

- 56 Breakfast Sandwich Recipes: Irresistible Sandwich Ideas to Kickstart Your Morning

- 50 Holiday Dessert Recipes: Delectable Dessert Ideas For The Christmas Holidays And Other Special Occasions

- 51 Easter Dessert Ideas: Scrumptious Easter Recipes For Any Occasion

Get the latest update on new releases from the author at:

https://www.brianneheaton.com/newsletter

About the Author – Brianne Heaton

Brianne Heaton started off collecting recipes that her family and friends enjoyed. After receiving many requests for copies of the recipes, she decided to share them by writing recipes books that everyone would appreciate.

Connect with Brianne Heaton

I really appreciate you reading my book! Here is my social media contact information:

Friend me on Facebook: https://www.facebook.com/BrianneHeatonRecipeBooks/

Follow me on Twitter: https://twitter.com/brianneheaton

Check me out on Goodreads: https://www.goodreads.com/author/show/8121938.Brianne_Heaton

Subscribe to my newsletter: https://www.brianneheaton.com/newsletter/

Visit my website: https://www.brianneheaton.com/

www.ingramcontent.com/pod-product-compliance
Lightning Source LLC
Chambersburg PA
CBHW061203010526
44110CB00064B/2667